GORDON WEST was born in 1896. He studied at the London School of Economics and served in the Royal Navy in the First World War. After the war he began a career in journalism, at one time working as Editor of Publications for the Liberal party. He also toured the United States with two presidential candidates in 1928 — Alfred E. Smith and Herbert Hoover — in order to study the progress of American elections for Lloyd George.

In the 1920s he was Foreign Correspondent for the *Westminster Gazette*, and during the years of the Second World War he was Foreign Editor of the *Daily Sketch*.

It was in the late 1920s that Gordon West and Mary, his wife, decided to explore the little-known island of Majorca, which was the inspiration for *Jogging Round Majorca*. In the 1930s they set off on their journey through Morocco, as a result of which *By Bus to the Sahara* was written.

Also by Gordon West

JOGGING ROUND MAJORCA

and published by Black Swan

BY BUS TO THE SAHARA

GORDON WEST

BLACK SWAN

BY BUS TO THE SAHARA
A BLACK SWAN BOOK : 0 552 99666 1

Originally published in Great Britain by
The Travel Book Club

PRINTING HISTORY
The Travel Book Club edition published in the 1930s
Black Swan edition published 1996

This Black Swan printing
Copyright © Transworld Publishers Ltd, 1996

**We are delighted to be publishing our Black Swan
edition of this charming book and whilst every effort
has been made to discover the owner of the work,
without success, we would be pleased to hear
from the Author's estate.**

Set in 12½/12pt Monotype Garamond by
Kestrel Data, Exeter

Black Swan Books are published by Transworld Publishers Ltd,
61–63 Uxbridge Road, London W5 5SA,
in Australia by Transworld Publishers (Australia) Pty Ltd,
15–25 Helles Avenue, Moorebank, NSW 2170
and in New Zealand by Transworld Publishers (NZ) Ltd,
3 William Pickering Drive, Albany, Auckland.

Reproduced, printed and bound in Great Britain by
Cox & Wyman Ltd, Reading, Berks.

TO MY WIFE
The Spirit of Joy,
who
paves the rough tracks
with Laughter
and finds
Diamonds in Dustheaps.

CONTENTS.

CONTENTS—*continued*

Live satisfied with Little, and
thou shalt be a king —

ARAB PROVERB

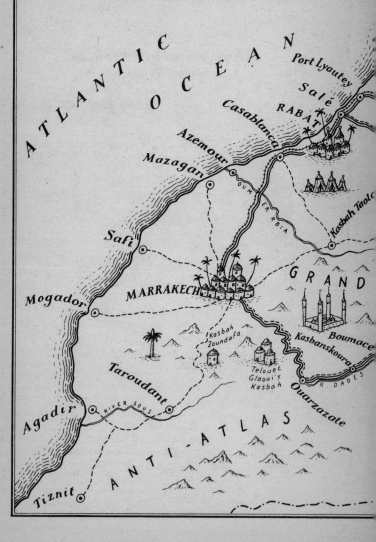

MOROCCO

from LONDON

ATLANTIC OCEAN

Port Lyautey
Salé
RABAT
Casablanca
Azemour
Mazagan
OUM ER RBIA
Kasbah Taol

Safi

Mogador

MARRAKECH

GRAND

Kasbah Zoundafa

Kasbanskoura

Telouet Glaoui's Kasbah

Boumace

R. DADES

Ouarzazate

Taroudant

Agadir
RIVER SOUS

ANTI-ATLAS

Tiznit

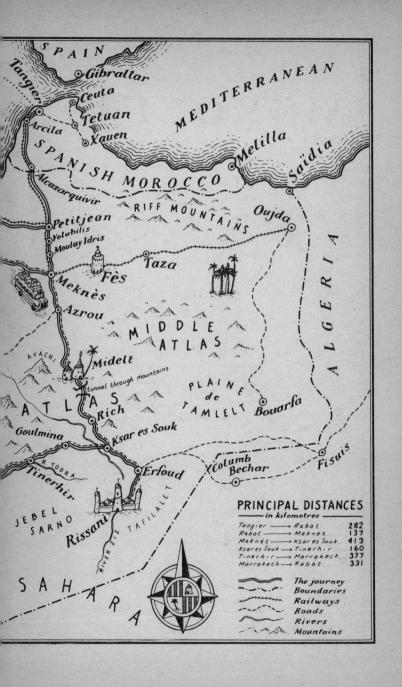

SPAIN

Tangier
Gibraltar
Ceuta
Tetuan
Arcila
Xauen

MEDITERRANEAN

Melilla
Saïdia

SPANISH MOROCCO

Alcazarquivir

RIFF MOUNTAINS
Oujda

Petitjean
Volubilis
Moulay Idris
Fès
Taza

Meknès
Azrou

MIDDLE
ATLAS

A L G E R I A

AYACHI
Midelt

Tunnel through mountains

PLAINE
de
TAMLELT

Bouarfa

A T L A S
Rich

Goulmina
Ksar es Souk

R TODRA
Tinerhir

Erfoud
Columb
Bechar
Fisuis

JEBEL
SARNO
Rissani

RIVER ZIZ TAFILALET

S A H A R A

PRINCIPAL DISTANCES
in kilometres

Tangier ⟶ Rabat		282
Rabat ⟶ Meknès		137
Meknès ⟶ Ksar es Souk		413
Ksar es Souk ⟶ Tinerhir		160
Tinerhir ⟶ Marrakech		377
Marrakech ⟶ Rabat		331

The journey
Boundaries
Railways
Roads
Rivers
Mountains

Tells of the Genesis of a Journey — the Power of a Grape-fruit — the Pursuit of a Bus by Train and Ship.

I

Now it may have been the pale face of winter London or the sameness of the social round or the chilly depths of the morning grape-fruit into which she meditatively gazed that prompted the artist, whom I will call the Spirit of Joy, to say how nice it would be to go to the Sahara by bus : I suspect the grape-fruit.

For I know that when she expresses herself while meditating thus, she is like the crystal-gazer glimpsing the future in a globe.

I agreed that it would indeed be pleasant, as were all improbable dreams ; and wondered how she proposed to find out where buses started for the Sahara and what were their times of departure. Now it is notorious that prophets, in their moments of revelation, are invariably without a sense of humour, so that my gentle irony fell on stony ground.

"This is the age of buses," proclaimed the prophet. "They run everywhere, even to Whipsnade. It was revealed to me recently by one Reuter, in a newspaper, that a bus now goes across the Andes. Perhaps I should say that it began to go across the Andes, until it had a misunderstanding about a precipice, to its detriment. Still, it was proof that buses do run almost everywhere ; so why not to the Sahara ?"

That a bus had fallen over a precipice in South America certainly seemed to confirm her belief in the ubiquity of buses ; so for a while we debated the charms of this mode of travelling to the African desert, assuming its possibility. From the grape-fruit came visions of an omnibus ploughing its way through sandstorms, skirting the palm-fringed glitter of oases and encountering those white-robed horsemen who in song are forever saying farewell to their steeds. But when the visions had faded and the world of reality reasserted itself, I inquired of the Spirit where she proposed to find out if her dreams could be realised.

"The best way would be to cross Morocco," she enlightened me. "Morocco belongs mostly to the French. We have a friend at the French Embassy. Let us ask him."

So together we went to the friend, asking him if they had any buses to the Sahara, and whether it would be pleasant to travel by them if they had.

Oh yes, he said, they had some very good buses, with drivers whose skill and reliability were beyond reproach. And he was sure we should travel in safety, because the dissidents — charming French euphemism for rebels who are robbers, cut-throats and murderers — were now so well in hand that they had neither robbed nor killed anybody for quite a time, indeed for several months.

For you must know that the southern areas of Morocco through which we would have to pass, over the High Atlas mountains to the burning plains beyond, had been subdued only four years before by French soldiers in a mountain war that cost many lives. Before that time, the Berber tribes of the Atlas had for three thousand years or more resisted all comers. Not even the Romans of old could conquer these primitive white men of North Africa, who from their inaccessibility had been for ever free to descend for pillage, murder and the waylaying of travellers. You will understand that it must be hard for men who have been used to cutting throats for three-thousand years to be asked suddenly to give up their hobby.

Our friend told us that we would find these savage men most friendly and charming, though he thought there might be some places where we should not go alone. But of these he could not tell us: it would be a matter for people in high places to warn us when we reached the country. And in the matter of buses, well, he began to have a small doubt as to whether it would be the best way to travel. In the South, he believed, they were used almost exclusively by the natives, and he thought that going native might not appeal to us. We reassured him that we liked nothing better, but it seemed that he still had doubts. A private car, now, he suggested . . . though in all frankness he had to admit that some of the regions through which we must pass had nothing to offer but rocky desert tracks which were not very good for a car . . .

But already he had gone too far. He had admitted the existence of buses to the Sahara; he had given substance to the vision of the grape-fruit; he had fuelled the small flame of wanderlust reborn that April morning. And presently, with his good wishes and assurances and a letter of introduction to the Residency of Morocco, we left him with grateful thanks and rising enthusiasm. We bought a map and went home to plan this journey to desert lands, through the country known to the Arabians as Mogreb el Aksar, or Land of the Furthest West; land of sunshine, palm groves and oases, of mosques and muezzins and the ancient walled cities of an Empire that died because it fostered those most perilous of national vices — exclusiveness and intolerance.

And if you come this journey with us and do not care for it, please do not lay the blame on us. Blame the grape-fruit.

2

We thought it a pity that before we could take a bus to the Sahara we had first to take a train and a boat in order to catch the bus; it would have been so much more to our liking to step aboard at say Piccadilly Circus and set off without the tribulations that attend modern luxury travelling. Although by persistent enquiry we had discovered that we could indeed travel by bus a greater part of the way from London, exclusive of the English Channel and a short section of the Mediterranean, time did not permit this adventure. So the train and the ship claimed us.

The East began to assert itself the morning we reached St. Pancras. The grimy departure platform was littered with sierras of luggage bearing the well-preserved labels of half the hotels of India and Burma and Shanghai and Australia; for the *Viceroy of India*, the liner on which we were to leave London's own port of Tilbury, first stop Tangier, would continue its way half round the world after it had deposited us in Morocco. So you will understand why the grim platform at the station looked to us quite like a British Empire in concentrated form.

Elderly men with dark reddish faces, looking almost as explosive as Signor Mussolini, trekked among the mountains of luggage, dangling sun-helmets from one hand while with the other they pointed out this and that piece of baggage to porters whose imperturbability suggested that they too might have assimilated something of the East. Hindu gentlemen stand at the doors of compartments or stroll the platform, watching the flurry of their rulers with calm eyes that tell nothing of their thoughts. Elderly mothers enjoy a last exchange of messages with thin-faced daughters returning to husbands in the remote places of the Empire. From first-class compartments elegantly languid women gaze with a cold consciousness of superiority and apparent lack of interest on a scene from which they seem entirely remote, as though it belonged to another world of which they are not a part. Stocky men with the stiff back and purposeful walk of non-commissioned officers in mufti laugh heartily with wives and sisters whom they as heartily kiss from the windows as the train moves out . . .

"What a blessing to see somebody really being human," sighed the Spirit as she observed this display of demonstrativeness which I am sure did not have the approval of the languid ladies and explosive men who were going out to hold the Empire together. We had dumped our luggage with ourselves in a second-class compartment where a sergeant's wife was telling two friends what a rare time they had down at dad's during the last week of leave. We had two suitcases, a large painting box and a five-feet long, sewn-up canvas bundle that resembled a body prepared for burial at sea, but was really a vast roll of artists canvas and a folding easel. Now this bundle, which herein-after we shall call "The Body," drew upon us from time to time a good deal of suspicion. And I must confess that it merited suspicion. It might well have been a body and it might equally well have been some kind of contraband. You will perhaps have observed that customs officials and hotel keepers are disposed to be inquisitive about sewn-up bundles shaped like bodies; and people in trains, after puzzling a while over the bundle, examine your face with special care for signs of an evil nature. Their suspicions are not allayed when they observe that you take precautions not to allow "The Body" out of your possession; for how can they know that it contains an artist's most precious possessions, without which life would have no meaning?

Now, although I was not the artist, I confess to a special affection for "The Body." For on the previous evening I had not only at the last minute ranged the shops of South Kensington in search of special twine with which to sew it up, but I had also at considerable trouble and expense provided some of its inner man. With the assistance of three shillings' worth of taxicab I had harassed innumerable shopkeepers at the verge of closing time in quest of a large can of special turpentine which the Spirit was sure would not be procurable in desert regions. I had gone, too, in quest of a folding stool for desert use, and of such mysteries as megilp and gouache, all of which were now part of "The Body's" interior.

Then there had been the business of soothing the Spirit and assuring her that she looked much more charming with her hair short than long. For you must know that she has long and luxuriant auburn hair of which she is not a little proud; but because desert places do not offer the amenities of the dressing table, she had been urged against her will to have her tresses cut a little. And she had returned from the hairdresser in despair and almost in tears. They had shorn her, they had ruined her hair, they had cut off at least three inches of it. Yet such are the persuasive powers of flattery that by the time the train was nearing Tilbury she had almost forgotten her lost tresses.

She had completely forgotten them after she had clutched my arm suddenly, pointed from the window and asked how on earth those liners had got into the green fields. Although she has wandered the world a good deal, she had never yet seen Tilbury; and the traveller's first impression of the port is a strange one. Here is the river Thames, next to it the railway on which you are travelling, and beyond that lie expanses of green land from which vast liners tower. Not until you are aboard do you realise how far inland from the river lie the docks.

When we alight from the train the East very definitely takes control. We are greeted by a parade of Indians, servants of the steamship company, and they are wearing clothes of blue with turbans of checked blue and white, of mustard and wine and of pink. They come forward with the curiously slow, bent-kneed and unhurried movement of the lascar, which is a glide rather than a walk. They are oddly out of place in the grubby barrenness of the docks. One of them wordlessly straps our two cases and the painting box over shoulders that look much too frail for the load, and glances at us with what seems to be reproach because I, having been well instructed in this matter, decline to let him also take " The Body."

And so we are up the long gangway and aboard, and a steward leads us to our cabin, where we are received by another steward who in greeting makes a little murmur of sound like a sleepy cat; our luggage is stowed with " The Body" under our bunks, and we are out on deck again to see the farewells from the dockside a long, long way below. So high we ride above the dock that the Spirit momentarily shrinks from leaning on the rails for fear she will topple the ship over . . .

The gangways are down and the last farewells are passing from below: the " don't-forget-to-writes" and the " have-a-good-times" which always cover the embarrassment of an English farewell at train or boatside. Yet from a boat the embarrassment is never so great, perhaps because of the greater distance that separates the seer-off from the departing friend. You do not, as at a train farewell, stand two feet from each other trying without much success to think of something to say which hasn't been said before; knowing that in the hearts of each is a wish that the train would hurry and consummate the parting, since it has to be made.

There is a good crowd of other people's friends and relatives to see us off. We divide them into two types, the cheerful ones and the tearful ones. The cheerful ones are determined to be bright till the end; the tearful ones just do not care if they do make sights of themselves. Here is one young woman who is a particularly determined weeper. She stands with her mother, who is holding a baby. She wears spectacles, and looks up forlornly to a young man who leans out from the second-class deck below and whom we think is a clerk returning to his job in the East. Her nose is red and the tears run unrestrainedly from beneath her spectacles down her pale cheeks.

"Let me 'old your glasses, duck," says mother, removing a hand from the baby and with a quick expert twist unhooking the intrusive objects from her daughter's ears. "There, now," she adds with satisfaction, as though to say, "Now you can have a good cry and nothing to stop you."

"Don't forget to write," quavers Duck irrelevantly, as though the young husband could possibly forget since he takes with him the memory of that pathetically tearful face.

There are other tearful faces and we see that their tears are all directed to the second-class and steerage voyagers, who lean and peer from the decks below. There is nobody to cry for the first-class passengers, nor is there anybody to wave them farewell. You see, when you feel responsible for holding an Empire together, you are reluctant to show any emotion, which is a weakness to be severely discouraged. So we who have paid a little more to travel glide from the dock unwept-for and unwaved-to, and those who have paid less feel as though their departure really matters to someone.

Two figures follow the great liner along the quay to the end as she makes her exit and swings slowly out into the water. One is a large and majestic policeman wheeling a bicycle. He walks protectively beside the monstrous bulk of the ship to the end of the quay, watches her swing out into the river, then turns and mounts his bicycle and cycles away to his tea with the air of one who has done his job and done it well.

He leaves at the end of the quay the dwindling figure of the young woman in spectacles, who has followed as far as she can without going into the water. As the *Viceroy of India* swings round the bend in the river and heads for the sea and the far places of the world, the young woman raises on high a small white bundle, her baby. I wondered if anybody else who might have been watching saw the bigger significance of that last gesture.

3

We are travelling first-class for two reasons. One is that we are a little tired after a winter of hard work in London and need rest in luxury. The other is that the weather is not good, we are indifferent sailors, and the Spirit says it is perhaps less trying to be sick first-class than second. The fare to Tangier is nine pounds, and we could have gone second-class for six. We decide that after we have gained strength from the African sun we shall return in the second-class, because we prefer its friendlier humanity to the formality of the first.

And now we have before us three and a half days of freedom, wherein we can indulge any whim that touches our fancy. We can stay in our bunks all day or laze reading in deck chairs swathed in rugs; or we can indulge to excess in the rich foods provided, to the end that we must spend the rest of our time strenuously playing deck games to counteract the effects of four large meals a day.

Then there is that other popular pastime, played by pairs, of sitting together on deck or in lounge, observing passing fellow-passengers, and turning your heads each towards the other to exchange significant glances, little tight-lipped smiles and murmured remarks. This is a game much favoured by the thinner and more elderly ladies returning to the East.

Or there is that more intriguing game of Spotting the Ship's Scandal. In this instance she is soon found. She is a lady of considerable title, gay, good-looking in middle age, and noted for her divorce; and her companion is a very young man who seems not to care tuppence if he does ruin his career in the Diplomatic Service, so great is his adoration.

Then there is the business of discovering whom to know and whom not. For ourselves, we do not care. We like a certain gay captain and that rare thing, a studious colonel who can talk on many subjects. We are puzzled by a charming young Spaniard, wondering why he so persistently advocates sherry as a drink, until we learn that he owns vineyards and wine presses in Granada and has been to London to advocate the greater consumption of his products. We hold aloof from the greyish mother with spinster daughter who without the necessary equipment makes vain attempts to be the life and soul of the ship. Best of all we like a troup of singing acrobats, a young Arab and his wife and a Spaniard with his brother, who have just left a London theatre for a tour of the Antipodes. Here is naturalness and spontaneous gaiety, and we are soon good friends.

And soon, after rough seas, the dreaded Bay of Biscay is passed, calm as the mind of a nun, and the captains and colonels are scanning the mountains of Spain through telescopes in vain search for signs of war. On the fourth morning we are awakened at dawn to a ship whose engines are silent, by a steward who nods to the porthole and murmurs: "Tangier." I peer out, seeing no colourful Africa, no palms and white houses in the sun, but a grey curtain like steel.

Forgive me if I introduce a topic without which no English discourse can be complete: I will say it in a whisper . . .

It was raining cats and dogs.

CHAPTER 2.

Tells of an African Greeting — the Ways of Charlie Abdullah — a Garden of Dreams — Sir John Lavery's Cook — the Englishwoman who married an Arab Leader — the Perfidy of Abkadar.

I

Now Africa, when it rains, can be very wet indeed ; and the rain that beats upon the ship like bullets and hisses into the grey sea is the best sort of African rain. But it is soon over, and before the tender is ready to take us the half-mile or so to shore, Morocco and its sunshine is all around us.

Across the water from the white town on the hill come a multitude of objects that look at first like gigantic coloured water-beetles but prove as they draw near to be Arab boats laden with merchandise. In a few minutes they have surrounded the ship, more than twenty of them, swaying on the waves that have now changed miraculously from grey to azure, spreading before us the coloured wares of Morocco. Each boat contains two Arabs, the oarsman and the salesman. While the oarsman keeps the boat in position the salesman throws up fifty feet of line, shouting to the passengers to tie it to the ship's rail. Soon a score of lines reach from boats to ship.

Then begins a hoarse clamour of salesmanship such as you have never heard before . . . "Look, ladee, nice cusson cover, lovely bag-for-you, all for neely nothing, I give him away, yes, for seventy-franc-ten-shilling, alri', how mooch you give ? Eighty franc, cost me eighty franc, alri', seventy franc and I starve, sixty-five franc, how mooch you give ? Getaway, fifty no good, I starve and die, fifty-five franc . . ."

BY BUS TO THE SAHARA

From a score of throats comes this clamour as the salesmen hold up for inspection their bright green and red and magenta leathers, covers for pouffes, hand-bags, purses, rush bags and baskets woven in many colours, rugs made by Arabs in factories for a few pence a day. The salesmen do not expect us to pay the price they ask, they are always prepared to reduce it by half. When a bargain has been struck the goods are tied in a basket to the line and drawn up to the ship, and the passenger pays the price into the basket and sends it down.

And now amid the clamour a long, narrow stair is unfolded down the ship's side, and we pass sway-ingly down to the tender that rocks below. A gigantic Arab wearing a fez, yellow pantaloons and a magenta jacket hauls us aboard as he roars out instructions to an unseen colleague, and soon we pass through that vociferous ocean bargaining over blue seas to the shore.

Tangier always begins with Charlie, whom you must know. You cannot arrive in this international city, gateway to Morocco, without meeting Charlie. He came forward to greet us as we stepped ashore and stood waiting for the luggage tender. He is a graceful young Arab of twenty-five with a pleasant smiling face and an ingenuousness that is very much more apparent than real. He wears a red fez proclaiming the unmarried state and a red-brown *djellab* or cloak over tweed plus-fours. It is not long since we met in Spain, for Charlie, whose other name is Abdullah, is something of a wanderer. He shook our hands, then raised his own hand to his lips, after the fashion of the Arabs. He asked us how we did and said how very glad he was to see us again.

Charlie Abdullah is the son of a merchant who once knew luxury but died after the Arab passion for gambling had brought him to penury. So what should

Charlie Adbullah do but become a guide? Now being a guide is the ambition of a multitude of pestiferous young men of Tangier, who find that sustained work is not to their liking; but Charlie Abdullah is a guide with a difference. His charm and his manners and his five languages — two of which he learned by studying them at the cinemas — raise him from the rut.

There is nothing in Tangier that Charlie Abdullah cannot show you. He will introduce you to a consul, a secret political meeting, a place where you may buy forbidden hashish, or he will take you to what he calls a House of Beautiful Women, still with that smiling, graceful charm of his. And if at the hour of sunset he should suddenly ask your pardon, step into a quiet byway and sink to his knees with his forehead to the ground, you will know that he is only praying to Allah for any sins you may have committed under his guidance . . .

We deposit our cases in a barouche-like carriage sheltered by a white sun-awning and drawn by an animal whose appearance, says the Spirit, suggests that it was the steed to which the Arab said farewell. Soon we are clattering up the hilly modern streets to our hotel at the summit. It stands like a white palace in a garden such as you may have dreamed of but seldom seen. Clusters of great lilies rise from the ground to meet white, bell-like lilies that hang from the trees, amid masses of magenta and puce geraniums that have for background white walls half hidden by a blue foam of morning glory. It is a garden of peace and colour and dreams. An Arab gardener plays at work among the lilies; another Arab in a striped yellow and white *djellab* and white turban, stricken in years, sits against a wall in the shade smoking hashish in a minute pipe of red clay with a wooden stem two feet long. At the end of the garden is a terrace on the side of the hill, and beneath lies the lovely panorama of Tangier, white town of green-roofed mosques reaching to a calm blue sea. Far away through the faint haze of morning we see the coast of Spain, and to the right a far-off hump that is Gibraltar.

Here is a place for dalliance and dreams, where time seems to have died. The African thrush that sings on the acacia tree might be one of the birds of Celtic Rhianon, which sang so sweetly that a year passed as a minute and a lifetime like an hour. Up the white road that climbs from the town comes a straggle of white-robed figures, of donkeys laden with burdens twice as large as themselves. From a compound on the right rises faintly the sound of braying donkeys and the dissatisfied grunt of camels that have brought produce in to the market. And upon all dwells the burning radiance of the sun.

After we have settled our rooms and taken coffee served on the terrace by a soft-footed Arab wearing red pantaloons and a red fez, we set off down the hill to the town. It is still only nine o'clock, and the market of the Grand Socco is alive with business. Here you will find all the colour and romance of a market of the Orient, and sample some of its odours.

In the great tree-shaded triangle, a surging multitude of many colours plys its multitudinous trades. Veiled women swathed in white sit cross-legged in rows before their wares — before crimson hills of outsize tomatoes, giant green peas, lettuces like young shrubs, carrots twelve inches long. Only their eyes and their hands invite you to buy. Lumbering women of the Riff mountains, unveiled because they are Berbers, squat beneath rush hats the size of umbrellas, with their goods arrayed on the ground before them: round flat cheeses, a dozen eggs, flat pale loaves, jars of honey and smeen, which is a kind of curd used for cooking after long burial under the ground. Negroes offer toffees of terrifying colour — vivid purple and green and magenta — sticks of pink and yellow rock, sugared peanuts, doughnuts oozing fat. The Spirit, who has a child's love of eating pretty colours, buys twenty-five centimes worth of purple mystery, says after tasting that it is the best sweet she has eaten since schooldays, and tempts me to a bite. Then more veiled women, sitting amid a chaos of flowers. We may buy a big bouquet of roses for one franc fifty, which is about twopence; or a larger bouquet of a dozen arum lilies for threepence.

Turbanned men crouched before piles of red and yellow babouches, the heelless backless slipper that is the Arabs only footwear. Ragged peasants from the country argue interminably over the sale of bundles of grass which is their only wealth. More Riff women talk themselves into frenzies in their efforts to sell long rush mats which are the only beds these people know, and for the first time we realise the significance of the instruction, "take up thy bed and walk." There were no iron bedsteads in the days of Christ.

We are drawn towards a sound of violence and savagery. A Riff woman and an Arab are facing each other. From their lips come volumes of sound; their hands wave menacingly in each others face. We await the climax, anticipating bloodshed. But we are disappointed. They are arguing about price, the price is settled, and the Arab walks off with his cheaply-gotten bed under his arm.

From this chaos of movement and Babel of tongues we pass through a pale mauve Moorish gateway into the main street. And here the town loses its purely native character and becomes international. Spaniards and Frenchmen and Jews, Englishmen and Italians jostle through the crowded pavements between shops that are largely European in character. Here are the cafés where political factions meet and where quarrelsome Spaniards sometimes come to blows and knife-thrusts over the civil war that drags on a few miles away across the blue straits below the down. Here at one café is the corner table on the pavement which was the favourite seat of the famous Walter Harris, correspondent of *The Times*, who in the course of his work became captive of the great rebel Raisuli of the Riff.

The street dips to a hollow, then rises steeply up long cobbled stops to the ancient *kasbah*, high-walled fortress that was once the town's stronghold. Past white houses half hidden under cascades of purple bougainvillaea we enter a great gateway into cool narrow alleys where Moorish children play around a water fountain. And here we climb to the high wall and look down on the city and the bay, meditating on the troubled history that has been wrought here.

Romans of old fought for and held it, Vandals and Visigoths and Byzantines struggled in those blue waters and in the narrow alleys, the Spanish and the Portuguese took their turns of possession; the English received it as a present — and gave it away.

A charming present, we agree, recalling how our Charles the Second received it as a dowry when he married Catherine of Braganza the Portuguese beauty. Yet so much trouble did this present bring upon him, and so much money did it cost, and so annoyed was Parliament by all this bother and expense, that after twenty-three years the English, to save money, blew up half the place and sailed away, leaving it to the tender mercies of the great sadist Sultan Moulay Ismail of Meknes, of whose playful habits I shall tell you later. On some of the walls you may see still the rude remarks about the inhabitants, scored by Stuart soldiers before they left for home.

Perhaps it is as well, then, that after all its tribulations the Tangier Zone should be internationally ruled by a mixed government drawn from eight nations, of which the greatest are Britain, France and Spain . . .

We climb down from the thirty-feet high wall and pass on through narrow ways into the native town, where the streets are corridors and the shops caverns in walls, wherein Arab shopkeepers sit cross-legged before their wares. And here in one of these narrow ways we have our first encounter.

In a tiny shop that is half a studio sits a little old man. From his almost black skin we judge that he is half negro. He has a straggle of white beard, and he looks up with a gentle, half-shy smile as we pause at the doorway. We are surprised to see that he is painting, so we enter. As he rises to greet us he puts down a half-finished work in water-colours. The walls of his small shop are lined with paintings. They are scenes of Arab life, of weddings and feasts and fetes. The Spirit examines them with such enthusiasm that the old man asks in French if she also is an artist and she tells him yes.

"Then you will perhaps know Sir John Lavery?" he asked surprisingly.

"Why yes, do you know him, too?"

"Oh yes," says the old man, and there is pride in his voice. "It is through him that I too am an artist."

"But how is this?" she asks.

Eagerly the old man turns to a corner, fumbles among some papers in an old desk, and produces a faded envelope from which he draws a letter and hands it to us.

"It began long ago, because of this," he says; and we read a note on paper headed from Sir John's address off the Cromwell Road, dated July, 1914.

"This is to certify that Benali el Rubati was in my service as cook, was hard-working, capable and is worthy of a good situation. I can thoroughly recommend him . . . John Lavery."

Now we are indeed intrigued. Benali invites us to coffee and we squat on the floor with him to hear his story. He told us that many years ago, before the war, Sir John lived for a while in Tangier, where he had a house. (Now we knew this to be so; and if you should go to Birmingham Art Gallery you will see one of the pictures he painted here.) At that time Benali entered his service, and when Sir John returned to London, Benali came with him for a time.

Benali had no knowledge of painting, but the art fascinated him. When the chance offered, he would study Sir John's pictures as they progressed from the first brush-strokes to the finished work. What a fine thing, thought Benali the cook, to be able to transfer to canvas the fleeting beauty which the eye can see but cannot hold. In the privacy of his room he began to make tentative attempts to paint; but it was hard, for he did not know the elements.

One day Benali the cook was sitting cross-legged on the floor of the studio, where he had no right to be, when Lady Lavery found him. He apologised and tried to escape; but Lady Lavery was always interested in other people's interest in her husband's work, and before long she had uncovered her cook's aspirations.

" And then she began to tell me some of the secrets of Sir John's work, and the things that puzzled me she explained," says Benali. " She helped me to study this art which captures the world's beauty and keeps it. I went on with my painting, yet never thinking that I should come myself to be an artist.

" And when I left, before the war, her words to me were 'that I should go on painting.' I went on painting. Back in Morocco I was a cook, a shopkeeper until business was bad, a bank messenger; and when I was not working I painted. Now a little success has come to me in old age. Allah has been good."

All his days now old Benali sits painting his

water-colours in the small shop that is half a studio. When once he has made a picture to his liking, he copies it a dozen, a score of times, according to its popularity. By no means are they great art, but they are characteristic of the Arab mind that conceives them, and have a naivety and an atmosphere that gives them charm.

You will see them on the walls in many of the houses of Tangier. We discovered later that six of them hang in the bar lounge of the Villa de France where we are staying. Benali sells them at prices that range from five to forty francs. It is his only livelihood now, though a poor one; but this is of less concern to Benali than that he has achieved an ambition born years ago in Sir John's studio at Kensington.

We talk long, sitting here on his littered floor; and we part with a promise to meet Benali later, so that he may lead the Spirit to scenes which he says would be good for her brush to paint . . .

And now hunger draws our thoughts to food. We can hunt the regulation meal at the cafés in the main street, or go further afield to one of the hotels or restaurants. Or we can lunch as we stand at a native *kabob* bar, and so save the time we should otherwise spend on elaborate eating. Now a *kabob* bar is the snack luncheon counter of the Arab; you will find one in every street in all the old cities of Morocco. Inside his small cavernous shop the cook stands behind his counter, on which rests a hollow stone boat filled with glowing charcoal. Beside the cook is a heap of spiced mincemeat, another of liver and fat cut into pieces the size of a farthing, and a pile of skewers. On one skewer he threads alternate pieces of liver and fat; round another he moulds with his hand a roll of mince. He dips them in pepper, lays them across the boat and turns them over the red charcoal till they are cooked crisp and brown. Then he takes a small flat cake of bread, slits it at the side, drops in the hot grill, and hands it to you for fifty centimes, or three-farthings.

They are good, these *kabobs*. We repeat the order and consider ourselves well fed. We cross to another small native bar and stand with white-robed Moors and Berbers in striped *djellabs* while we are brewed a glass of mint tea, the national drink of the Moroccan. It is a sweet, refreshing drink, three glasses of which take the place of the cocktail before a ceremonial banquet. Pale china tea is poured boiling on to a handful of fresh mint leaves, whose flavour is given to the tea. We take a glass apiece and are refreshed and ready for further wandering.

2

And now we have some calls to pay before we plan our bus journey. First we have promised to visit the editor of the local English newspaper. It has the splendid-sounding name of *Tangier Gazette and Morocco Mail, incorporating El Moghreb Al Aksa and Morocco*. From this you must not assume that it is an elaborate production of the kind you have on the home break-fast table. It has eight pages recording the doings of the English in the Tangier Zone. It tells its news plainly and discreetly with less display even than the august *Times* of London.

We found the Editor in an arched cavern below street level. The open archway that serves as a door faces a piece of waste land coloured with white and yellow ox-eyed daisies. Two donkeys are tethered outside. As we sit before the editorial desk, discuss-ing this and that, the conversation is from time to time interrupted by violent braying from one of the donkeys.

"Damn that donkey," says the editor each time,

relieving his feelings by aiming a blow at an inoffensive fly with a swatter that lies on his desk.

It is no easy job, this editing in Tangier. The editor is also his own reporter and sub-editor and print supervisor and make-up expert; he has to take a hand even with the production. He leads us through a door into an adjoining cavern where the paper is printed. Two natives are busy, one setting a piece of news in print by hand, letter by letter, taking his type from a series of boxes; the other working the handpress on which the paper is printed a sheet at a time. It is a long and laborious process, little changed since Caxton first conceived the idea; and we part with a feeling that the editor deserves more credit than he probably receives for producing as neat a paper with so primitive an equipment.

Not far away is The Mountain, rising high above Tangier and its blue sea, where the English colony has made its home. Here live the Very Best People of the International Zone, the retired colonels and civil servants and men who have spent their lives in the far places of the world. They have brought with them their own civilisation to this paradise on the hill. They hunt and they shoot and they fish, stick pigs, play polo and indulge in every conceivable pastime that involves knocking, throwing, driving or otherwise propelling a ball. They are a close community, like all English colonies of their kind, living in these spacious white villas amid a discreet profusion of flowers. Do not imagine you can be on equal terms with them unless you have the very best of credentials. And if you should gain entry to their society, above all do not make reference to stories you may hear down in the town of how certain of their countrywomen have gone very wrong indeed with handsome Moors. They will not be able to deny it, but they can always play the ostrich . . .

3

You will have read in newspapers from time to time of English girls who have found romance and given themselves in marriage to eastern princes and Oriental sheikhs. And you will no doubt have shaken your heads and wondered, as we have wondered, about the ultimate fate of their romances and whether they would find happiness.

Now in Tangier we have discovered one English-woman who above all others should be able to provide an answer to these questions, for in her youth she experienced such a marriage. We are on our way to see her now, with a letter of introduction from London.

It was in 1873 that Emily Keene, twenty-two years old, fair-haired daughter of a Surrey family, met and married Hadj Abdeslam ben Alarbi, Grand Shareef of Wazzan the Holy City. She was a governess, he a descendant of the Prophet Mahomet — no wild, tent-dwelling *sheikh* of the desert of fiction, but a handsome cultured Moor whose family was once so powerful that Sultans could not be chosen without its sanction. As a descendant of Mahomet and of a long line of holy men, he was head of a religious order venerated all through the lands of the Moslems.

Now because he admired the English it was his desire to marry an Englishwoman, so he offered to divorce his three wives — a simple matter among the Moslems — and sought marriage with Emily Keene. At first she refused, because of religious differences; but when she found that the Koran permitted such marriages she consented, to the despair of her parents, and was married to the Shareef at the British Legation in Tangier.

To reach her house we climbed the long steep mule

pathway past the *kasbah* to a high plateau known as The Marshan, a place of peaceful white villas in gardens brilliant with flowers. We have to ask our way, and so we meet Abkadar, a young student with a gentle smile and graceful manner, who volunteers to take us to the Shareefa, of whom he speaks with great veneration. He told us how, many years ago, she had brought vaccination to Morocco, saving hundreds of lives. The disease of the spots and the itch, he said, had been a curse in the country, and the people knew no way of preventing it. At first they feared vaccination, believing it some kind of devilry or witchcraft. But the Shareefa conquered their fears, and herself scratched with the needle many thousands of Arabs and Berbers who in time flocked to her house to be saved. Oh, yes, said Abkadar, the Shareefa was a grand lady of many friends and great renown.

We reach her house, a square white building near the road, on one side overlooking the blue Atlantic. As we walk down the wide open space that separates it from the next villa, we pass an elderly grey-bearded Moor of great dignity, in white robes, who paces up and down with his hands behind his back. His gaze is on the ground and he appears not to be aware of our passing; but Abkadar bows his head in reverence and when we are out of hearing says in a hoarse whisper that it was the Shareef, her son; for the Shareefa has been a widow for many years, and the son has succeeded the father.

We pass into a garden where crimson lilies grow and are received by a negress who takes in our card of introduction. While Abkadar waits, we are led into the house to a room which at a glance tells something of the story of a life, so strange a mixture is it of east and west, of an English taste long dead and a Moorish culture that has lived for centuries.

Moorish tapestries vie with fringed table-cloths of

nondescript colour on small Victorian mahogany tables set among carved Arab furniture of exquisite workmanship. Many ornaments of Moorish design and pattern, bowls and pots of copper and brass, stand on tables and mantelpiece; pictures of relations and friends in frames of red plush and silver adorn walls and stand in any convenient place. It is the room of one who has not been able or willing to submerge all that belonged to a civilisation she has forsaken.

Into the room comes quietly a boy of fifteen or so. He wears a light grey robe and his face is of the very pale brown colour of the cultured Moor. He greets us with a quiet dignity as he shakes hands and explains that his grandmother the Shareefa is prepared to receive us. We are led to another room, and here, by the window in an armchair covered with an antimacassar, sits the woman who sixty-five years ago scandalised her friends by marrying an Arab.

She is a white-haired wrinkled old lady nearing ninety now, still with the blue eyes that went with the fair hair of Emily Keene of so long ago. She wears the clothes that our grandmothers wore, with a woollen shawl over her shoulders. Her voice is still strong, her mouth firm and with a suggestion of humour. She is feeling not very well to-day, she says, so we will forgive her if she does not talk for long. She questions us about ourselves, about our work and our opinion of Morocco, and we can see that she loves this country of her adoption. Of the country she abandoned she never speaks, it seems to have little interest for her. We think that perhaps in her old age it has receded too far into the past and become like a half-remembered dream.

And then, in response to our discreet questions, she tells us a little of her own past. Her life has not been without adventure. Times were when the Shareef, as ambassador of the Sultan, made long journeys on horseback into the wild south to treat with turbulent tribes, and his wife accompanied him with their retainers, riding like a man and aiding him in his work. She was not relegated to the inferior place of most Moslem wives and kept in jealous confinement; she lived a full life and saw many strange sights denied to wives of the harem. But more important to her than these things was her work for the people. "Romance — yes, that was the real romance," she says. "To learn the ways and customs of the people and to help them. If I had my life over again, I would choose no better way of spending it."

Of course the Spirit had to ask her if her life had been happy. She smiled. "As happy as most lives, happier than many," she answered. "But you do not expect perpetual sunshine without shadow, even in Morocco."

Afterwards we learned what some of those shadows had been : how in later years the Shareef had broken his vow of monogamy and married other wives, one of them a former slave; and how he had developed a mental trouble in which the Shareefa had nursed him till he died. Yet these things did not turn Emily Keene from her purpose of making their marriage a success; and you will realise how broadminded a woman she was when I tell you that three of her best friends were the wives whom the Shareef had divorced.

When we are preparing to depart we glance at a photographic group on a table — of bearded Moors with strong, pondering faces and youths with calm intelligent eyes.

"My sons and grandsons," she murmurs. "Such fine men, such splendid boys". . .

Here then is our glimpse of the woman who defied convention and race and religious prejudice by marrying one whom the newspapers delight to call a sheikh; and you may judge for yourselves whether she was justified in her choice . . .

Abkadar the student was waiting for us with a smile when we went out into the sunlight.

"You would now perhaps like a glass of tea," he said.

Together we walked down the hill to the entrance of the Kasbah. On the opposite side of the road, beside a building bright with blue Moorish tiles, we entered a garden of white stone festooned with purple bougainvillaea. On the other side of the enclosure in an alcove, four Arabs were squatting on a rush mat round a game of cards. Sometimes a burst of laughter rose above the murmur of their voices. From a distance we could hear the shriller sound of many boyish voices repeating parrot-like the lessons of the Koran. Abkadar said there was a school round the corner.

The café keeper, an Arab friend of Abkadar, placed glasses of fragrant sweet mint tea before us. We sat for a long time, while the Spirit sketched and Abkadar told us of his home and his sisters, and pulled open his djellab to show us the trousers one of his sisters had made. He wore a little white knitted skull-cap, which had been made by another sister.

When we rose to go, he asked us for his pay.

Now you will agree that it is a shock to find that one whom you thought had been your friend for the afternoon suddenly reveals a mercenary motive for his friendship. And the shock is the greater when your friend had been so gentle and charming, displaying a degree of culture that you do not find in the ordinary Arab youth of the streets. Yet here was the charming Abkadar asking for money. The truth is that you cannot trust the young Arab of the towns not to have been bitten by the passion for acting as a guide.

He wanted twenty francs. We pointed out to him

that it was not usual for money to pass between friends in this way. He answered mournfully, saying this was indeed sad, but it would be sadder still if he should not be able to go on with his studies because we would not pay him his due.

We decided to give him his francs, but because he had disappointed us we will play with him a little first.

We point out that we did not engage a guide. Abkadar's eyes open wide and he says that, since he guided us, he must be a guide, how could we think he was doing anything but be a guide?

Anyway, we say, if we pay him, it will be the end of our friendship, which cannot survive money payments.

He rolls his head mournfully. Friendship, he says, is a precious thing, but francs are necessary for life, and how can there be friendship without life? Without the twenty francs that were his by right, he intimated in a fine flow of language, he would surely soon be starving, his studies would end, his sisters would sit sad-eyed and haggard in their home and his mother would spend her days weeping for their fading beauty and health, for she would know that they could never have husbands; they would surely die and his mother would go every Friday to the cemetery to sit by their graves. Oh, the tragedy in the eyes of Abkadar, oh, the despairing droop of his young shoulders, oh, the miseries to come, the bitter shame and sorrow because we would not give him those twenty francs.

Only when we burst into laughter did he know he had won. The sorrow fell from him like a cloak and he glowed with renewed friendship as he took the money. He would be our friend for ever, he said, he would remember us in his prayers.

"Don't forget your commission on the tea," the Spirit unnecesssarily reminded him; for every Arab in the cities of Morocco takes his ten per cent. On anything he induces you to buy in shop or café.

Abkadar looked wistfully at the empty glasses.

"It is no more than thirty centimes," he said, and, brightening, added, "You have a long walk and need much refreshment, will you not have some more tea before you go?"

As the shoulders began to droop once more we parted. When we turned at the café gateway, Abkadar was sitting cross-legged in the circle of card-players, our twenty francs in his hand, his suffering sisters, if they existed, forgotten . . .

It is twilight when we pass through the Grand Socco on our way to the Villa de France. Many of the market people still sat like shrouded ghosts on the ground beside unsold wares, lighting them with pieces of candle and oil flares. The exciting vibration of a multitude of drums fills the air, for the snake-charmers and the story-tellers and the conjurers have arrived, each sitting with his circle of audience in the dim light. Higher up the hill, in an enclosure which is the charcoal mart, hooded figures crouch before candles in improvised tents of sacking in which they will spend the night. A camel carrying half a haystack on its back strides slowly past us, contemptuously aloof. In the fondouk at the bottom of our hotel garden there is a hoarse grumbling of camels gone to their rest and the occasional braying of an ass. An old blind Arab who sits all day on the steps leading up to the paradise garden has nodded to sleep.

We dine to-night in a long, cool hall of white and crimson, served by silent-treading Arabs in voluminous black trousers and red fezes. And when later we go out to the flower-scented terrace and look down on the town, white under the moon, there is no sound but the faint grumbling of camels and the distant rapid throbbing of a single drum. Tunk-a-*tunk*-a-tunk-*tunk*, tunk-a-*tunk*-a-tunk-*tunk*.

CHAPTER 3.

*Tells of Troublesome Advisers — Journey through Paradise
— Memories of Raisuli the Bandit — the Loveliness of
Rabat — Lyautey's Achievement.*

I

There comes a morning when we begin to plan
for the journey across Morocco to the south; and at
once our difficulties begin. Perhaps they are not so
much difficulties as artificial barriers which everybody
raises when we express an intention to undertake
something which others have not experienced.

Now from the number and variety of the warnings
we received against carrying out the journey on which
we had set our hearts, we might have been a pair of
Marco Polos starting on an adventure from which
there could be no return.

It began with the travel agency on whom we called
in search of bus routes. The expert looked at us oddly
for a moment and said that of course we knew there
was an outbreak of a certain dangerous epidemic in
one of the places we proposed to visit? He would not
advise us to go by bus, because further south we
should be travelling alone with the natives, a thing
which was not done by Europeans. He advised a
private car, which would prevent our coming into
contact with possible danger.

We thanked him and asked for the bus connec-
tions. He could not give us them beyond a certain
point, after which, he thought, they did not run. In
certain of the obscure villages there would be nowhere
for us to stay. Moreover, to cross one territory we
should have to go first to Marrakech and obtain a
permit from the military. No doubt he did his best,

but he was not helpful. We discovered later that his information was wrong in every particular: he was at least a year out of date.

Others also warned us of the innumerable annoyances and perils we should face. At the British consulate, a lovely white Moorish villa in a garden of jasmine and lilies and geraniums, we had other warnings; and as we walked up the road, having obtained our visas to cross the war zone of Spanish Morocco, one of the Consul's young men ran out after us to add still another warning.

Then we were told by others that we must take a medicine chest and a supply of tinned food and plenty of insect powder and a weapon of some kind for defensive purposes; practically no luggage because we should be robbed, lots of heavy clothes because we should be cold, only light clothes because we should be burnt up, sun helmets because we were sure to get sunstroke, an escort when we passed beyond the Grand Atlas mountains: until the Spirit gently asked one distressing informant if it would not be as well to take also a pair of coffins so that we could be sure of decent burial.

Now we have wandered in many odd places of the world, and we know that the stories of perils and discomforts told beforehand by those who have never experienced them are invariably inaccurate. These foreboders are like the man who knows Government secrets because he has a nephew whose fiancée's mother's cook has a sister whose young man served Downing Street with milk. They relate distorted stories of isolated incidents told by others who have heard them from somebody else. They hear of a man being bitten by an adder in some remote part of Morocco, and soon they infest a hundred square miles of territory with cobras.

So we pay no heed to these Edgar Allen Poe

story-tellers, these Dickensian Fat Boy terrorists. We
continue with our plans. Only in one particular do
we give way : we decide to cross the Spanish Zone to
the French territory by train instead of bus. For we
found there was truth in the stories we heard of this
region. Spanish Morocco is on a war footing, young
men of Franco persuasion are arrogant with newly-
won power, buses are held up and searched at any
time and in any place, and many a traveller has lost
his money and possessions. Buses are vulnerable ; but
trains, carrying armed guards and gendarmerie, are
free from interference.

So at seven o'clock on a sunny morning we trundle
down the hill to the railway station in our old friend
the barouche with the white awning. We have one
small handcase with a change of underclothes, the
painting box, and of course, "The Body.". When
the carriage draws up at the small bare station by the
blue bay of Tangier, a rabble of Arab youths surround
it, and before we have stopped one of them has
whipped out "The Body" and is making towards the
station.

A shrill cry and a vehement order from the Spirit
arrest him and he explains in voluble French that he
is a porter who wants to carry our luggage and doesn't
wish that we should miss the train. The Spirit insists
again so vehemently upon his leaving "The Body"
alone that she draws upon the unfortunate corpse the
curiosity of other Arabs, who begin to be convinced
that there must be something very queer indeed about
this queer-looking object. A negro boy gives it a
surreptitious poke with his bare foot and hedges away
from it. The group of clamorous would-be porters
make way as I swing it towards them ; they perhaps
fear that its contact might carry a curse.

And now we are in the train, bound for Rabat, the
seat of French Government of Morocco, on the other

BY BUS TO THE SAHARA

side of the Spanish Zone. It is a small and unobtrusive
train, with an old-fashioned type of steam engine and
four coaches, first, second, third and fourth class.
This last is for the poorer Arabs, who may travel at
a fare of about six miles for a penny, in a coach
resembling a covered luggage van with windows. A
few benches line the sides, and when these are
occupied the travellers sit cross-legged on the floor,
which is no hardship for an Arab. When the train
starts, only two white-cloaked figures sit swaying in
the bare wooden coach; but before we have travelled
ten miles it is crowded. From its windows one or two
women in white, veiled to the eyes, gaze out like nuns
at a passing world of beauty in which they may not
reveal whatever charms their faces possess. We find
it amusing to speculate on these hidden faces and try
to imagine from the qualities of the eyes what the rest
of the face may be like. Sometimes, in the eyes of
women who stand veiled at the stations into which
we jerkily clatter, we see a loveliness that makes us
want to risk assassination by pulling down the veil.
And we meditate on this strange custom, born of one
man's jealousy of his fourteen wives. For it was
Mahomet's jealousy thirteen hundred years ago which
causes these women to hide their beauty today. The
ancient tribes of Arabia had no thought of concealing
the beauty of their wives until the ageing Prophet,
perhaps growing less sure of his powers to charm,
decreed that his own women should modestly conceal
their faces when they went abroad in Medina so that
other men should not be tempted. The fashionable
people of Medina of that time were like fashionable people of every age: they liked to imitate the
highest in the land. So the women copied the wives
of Mahomet the leader, and the lesser people imitated
the fashionable until the whole of Arabian woman-
hood hid its face from public gaze. The Prophet made

no religious decree about the veiling of women; he created a fashion which has become part of a religion.

They make lovely pictures of mystery, these veiled women in white, as they stand on the station platforms. Their background could not have been better chosen. If you would visualise a Moroccan railway station, you must dissociate your thoughts from the grim, drab structures of brick and iron, glass roofs and grime to which we in the north are accustomed. Each station here is a paradise. At either side of the line a low built, snow-white building, flat-roofed in Moorish style, half hides itself beneath exuberant cascades of purple bougainvillaea. On the platforms you may stand in the shade of trees laden with acacia festoons, or gaze enchanted on the crimson blossoms of the hibiscus, while the perfume of jasmine comes to you through the train windows. Across the whiteness of the station building is painted in vivid blue the name of the village, and every name is an enchantment. Karia ben Aouda, Souk el Arba du Rharb, Oued Fouant, Ksar Arboaus: each tells you something of its special character. A *ksar* is a village, *oued* means a river, a *souk* is a market, and Arba is Wednesday.

The train passes through flat lands painted purple and rose and yellow with flowers. Sometimes a field of ox-eyed daisies extends as far as the eye can see, carrying your gaze over to the mountains of the Riff that crouch still and blue in the distance. An expanse of poppies burns red for miles in the sun. Camels graze in fields yellow with birdsfoot trefoil, where storks perch meditatively and large white cowbirds rest on the back of black cattle. An Arab walks on earth of burnt sienna behind a crude wooden plough of the kind that Abraham knew, pulled by a slow camel whose disdain for all around him surpasses anything that could be expressed by the most contemptuous of human beings.

We have a long wait at the frontier of the Tangier Zone where Spanish Morocco begins. There is a great to-do with passports and stampings and questionings as to our destination. Beside the station runs the road where the frontier barrier, a pole that is lifted when traffic has to pass, is guarded by two Franco sentries.

Here for the first time we have travelling companions — a Spanish father and mother of ample proportions with their daughter, a girl of perhaps eighteen, who has large lustrous dark eyes and Spanish-black hair. With them they bring an atmosphere of cheerful friendliness. They have no luggage, for they are not travelling far. They have none of the aloofness of the colonial French, whom we were later to find so uninterested in everything except themselves; and soon we are well on with a five-sided conversation. Because we are strangers and guests, they are solicitous for our comfort. They observe that the Spirit is feeling the heat, so to shield her the daughter pulls down the blinds. The Spirit thanks her and as an exchange of courtesy tells the mother what lovely eyes her daughter has. The mother beams and the daughter smiles and says, Ah, but the senora's hair, so lovely, so rare, and leans forward to caress it. So then the father and I exchange cigarettes and the mother presently brings from a capacious bag some sandwiches and fruit and a bottle of wine and insists that we share their meal. Thus a happy hour passes until our Spanish friends alight at Arcila with much handshaking and bon voyages and a promise from us that we will call on them if ever we stay in their town.

It was an invitation we would like to accept, for Arcila was the home of the great bandit Raisuli, whose palace still stands on a cliff by the sea. He had it built by novel methods. Under penalty of death if they

failed, every man living within fifty miles or so of
Arcila was compelled to bring twenty mud bricks and
incorporate them in the rising walls. By the time the
palace was finished more than five thousand men had
assisted in its building. Here Raisuli kept his hoard
of gold, won by robbery, the ransom of captives and
political chicanery.

This Raisuli, strange mixture of cruelty and culture, who was born a poor Berber, won for himself a
college education and returned to his native country
a brigand, was once in the running for the Sultanate
of Morocco. He was of the stuff of which many a
past Sultan was made. He held at bay the armies of
Spain and by his actions overthrew governments. He
raided a house in Tangier and walked off with a certain
Mr. Perdicarus of the United States. This brought
American battleships into the Bay of Tangier with
an instruction from Theodore Roosevelt to "get
Perdicarus alive or Raisuli dead." Yet Raisuli escaped
with a ransom of £14,000, laughing at the might of
battleships. He spent seven years in heavy chains in
the dungeons of Mogador and emerged to win for
himself the Governorship of Tangier from the man
who had imprisoned him. He played off European
governments one against the other. If the wild blood
that was in Raisuli had not conquered qualities of mind
which those who knew him say touched genius, he
might have died magnificently instead of in the
captivity of his rival Abd el Krim, himself now an
exiled rebel in Reunion.

To-day the Palace of the Eagle of Zinat and Sultan
of the Mountains, as they called Raisuli, lies empty
beside the white town that Phoenicians founded
long B.C. Ziliz they called it when the Goths took it
from the Romans. Then came our own Normans
in the eleventh century, fresh from their conquests in
England, and left only dead people amid the wreckage

of the once prosperous town. To-day the people of Arcila, 4,000 of whom are Moors, 500 Jews and 1,500 Spaniards, know only peace.

The train takes us now along the coast of the blue Atlantic, and away to the landward are the fields of colour and the storks. Sometimes we clatter past an Arab village of small round huts, their walls of pale yellow mud, their roofs cones of blue-grey straw, rising above a protective compound of giant cacti in yellow flower. Storks perch on the peaks of many of these cones, staring solemnly at our passing train and oblivious of any human activities below them: for the stork is a sacred bird and has no fear of man. He brings honour to the house on which he chooses to nest; if he should desert it, there are evil things in store for those who live beneath.

Soon we have passed Alcazarquivir, town of fourteen thousand Moslems, Jews and Spaniards, which in turn through the centuries has been Carthaginian, Greek and Roman. Its Arabian name is El Ksar el Kebir, which means the Village that is Big: one regrets that the Spaniards should have substituted so much less attractive a designation. From here we go far inland again, until we change trains at Petitjean, lunch at the station while we wait, and start off once more towards the coast, this time by swift electric train.

Since we lost our Spanish friends we have travelled alone. But at Port Lyautey, modern French town built no longer ago than 1913 and named after the great administrator whom the French have to thank for their successful colonisation of Morocco, we have a new companion. He is evidently a *caid*, local governor of the Moors. He is robed in white, with white muslin over his *djellab* and a magnificent white turban. The size of a Moor's turban is an indication of his importance. Penetrating brown eyes of a shrewd observer look from the pale brown face made venerable by a grey beard. He has an air of one accustomed to command. Two retainers, one a young negro, superintend his departure. They deposit his luggage of two expensive-looking modern suitcases in an adjoining compartment, where one remains to guard it. The negro who remains behind leans forward to kiss his master's shoulder before the train departs. We greet the *caid* with a " good day," which he returns courteously; but our hopes of further discourse are disappointed. He sits back with great dignity in his corner, produces from the voluminous folds of his clothes a magnificently bound volume of the Koran, and reads for the remainder of the journey. His lips move continuously and never once does he raise his eyes nor make any movement except to turn a page. Thus he remains for an hour or more until we enter Rabat, some eight hours after leaving Tangier.

2

The loveliness of Rabat begins with the railway station and ends only when you regretfully leave the city behind you. The train runs in and halts between two walls of a deep channel cut in red rock, on which exotic creepers hang their cascades of blossom. Two wide stone staircases curve up from the pair of platforms, leading to a great white stone hall whose fourth side, facing a street where the sunlight dazzled the eyes, consists of windows fourteen feet high, set in black wrought-ironwork on either side of wrought-iron-and-glass doors of palatial dimensions. Around the sides of the hall Arabs and Berbers in *djellabs* of white, mauve and yellow sit cross-legged against the walls, waiting with the imperturbable patience of the Orient for a train that may come in an hour, or three hours, or to-morrow — it matters little to the

Oriental mind. Arab travellers will arrive soon after dawn to catch a train that leaves at midday. One old woman sitting here as we pass has a cheap alarm clock on the floor at her side; she is fast asleep and her yashmak has immodestly fallen from her face, exposing her aged mouth; but she puts her trust in the clock and knows she will not miss her train.

We carry our scanty luggage through the palatial doors into an avenue whose whiteness in the glare of the sun is intolerable to the eyes. On the other side of the avenue we see a magnificent hotel, set behind a café garden where hibiscus blooms around blue tables set beneath orange-coloured sun umbrellas. We cross and enter a marble hall, dim and cool and semi-Moorish in style. Our handbags and 'The Body' are gently whisked away by be-fezzed Arab boys, we are greeted at the desk by a gentle, soft-spoken Moor, and in a few minutes find ourselves the tenants of a suite of two verandah rooms on the sixth floor, each with bath and shower, at a cost of three shillings a day. This, maintains the Spirit, is the peak of luxury before we begin the descending scale, for it is from Rabat that we are to start our travels by bus to more primitive regions.

After tea in the garden we set off with our introduction to M. Simoneau, of the Residency General. Our way takes us through the city which is the pride of French Morocco, as it was of its creator, the late General Lyautey. It was he who fashioned this place of beauty, planning its avenue and devising the style of its architecture. Like all the French cities of Morocco, built since the Protectorate was established some twenty-six years ago, it lies on the outskirts of a Moorish city of ancient times. Ancient Rabat el Fath, the Camp of Victory, was built by a great Sultan of the 12th century to commemorate

Moslem triumphs over the Christians in Spain. Modern Rabat celebrates the more pacific victory of French diplomacy and finance over the Moslems of to-day.

It is a commemoration worthy of a great achievement, which had made of Lyautey almost a patron saint of modern Morocco. It was in 1907 that he took the first step which led to this turbulent country passing under the protection of France. A year before, the Treaty of Algeciras had given France the right to build a harbour for trading at Casablanca, further down the coast. But the tribes revolted; they wanted no Christian incursion. They massacred the Jews, according to custom, and hemmed in the French at Casablanca. The trouble spread when Mulay Hafid, brother of the weak Sultan Abd el Aziz, revolted in Marrakesh and claimed the throne. Abd el Aziz appealed for help, and here was Lyautey's chance.

He offered Aziz aid in return for an extension of French influence. He guaranteed to protect Morocco's frontiers, to control the ports and re-organise the army. Abd el Aziz had no choice but to accept. But it was not until 1912 that France received a full protective treaty, granted by Mulay Hafid, successor to the brother who had been deposed by his people for selling his country to the French. Maréchal Lyautey became Resident-General, established his headquarters at Rabat and planned this city to house his Government.

In the twelve years of his enlightened dictatorship he created order out of chaos among the warring tribes. Year after year he penetrated into new territory and, having conquered it, won its friendship. "Respect consciences, flatter interests," was his motto. He respected tribal laws and customs and created markets for native goods and produce. Whenever he penetrated into new, unconquered territory, he erected a hospital at which his opponents could receive free treatment for wounds and illness — and return to the tribe when they were well to fight him again. Yet it was not until 1934, after his death, that the final conquest was made, when the savage Berber tribes of the Grand Atlas mountains in the south were brought into subjection after a hard and perilous campaign . . .

And now we are walking among the white palaces up the hill towards the Residency that was Lyautey's creation. Lofty date palms dreaming in the sun shade the wide avenues, exotic trees droop their mauve blossoms as you pass along the pavements. Between the palaces and the pavements grow hedges of blue verbena, crimson hibiscus and purple bougainvillaea. Eucalyptus trees shed their white blossoms in gardens. The headquarters of Posts and Telegraphs of Morocco has a white tower rising from a building half buried in purple blossom.

These buildings of the Government lie on one side of an avenue that climbs towards the Residency; and they are linked by a white stone pergola whereon grows wisteria and clematis. For a quarter of a mile this pergola mounts the hill, so that you may pass under its protection from the Department of Rivers and Forests to the Home Office, from the Foreign Office to the Bureau of Native Affairs. Can you imagine, asks the Spirit, our Ministers in Whitehall passing from their offices to a Cabinet Meeting at Downing Street under a pergola of flowers?

Through a white courtyard a Zouave in voluminous red trousers and blue tunic led me to Monsieur Simoneau. He is in charge of the propaganda and press for the Government. He sits in an office that looks out upon a flowery garden. He is a young man, dark-haired, with a quiet restful voice and a gentle manner. Over a cigarette we settle down to a talk.

He smiles as I repeat the stories we have been told of the horrors of the south.

" All those things are past," he says. " You will find it a most interesting journey — and you can go *all* the way to the Sahara by bus, if you do not mind a little rough travelling."

Before we part he has offered us Government passes that will take us anywhere by bus, introductions that we may use on our way, and an invitation to attend the Sultan's great fête of Mouloud, the birthday of Mahomet, if we return to Rabat by a certain date. This city of white palaces and flowers is one of the four Imperial Cities of the old Moroccan Empire, and on the Feast of Mouloud draws to itself all the caids and khalifas of the country to swear fealty and bring gifts to the Sultan. We should do well not to miss this celebration, says M. Simoneau.

We agree to return from the Sahara in time for the feast, say au revoir to M. Simoneau beneath the Government pergola and wander down the hill in the cool of evening to search for a meal.

Now there are many things to tell of Rabat and its ancient glories, but I shall reserve them until we return for the Sultan's party.

CHAPTER 4.

Tells of a Journey by Bus — House of the Swallows — the Playful Ways of Ismail the Sadist — City of the Monster — Strange Entertainment — Sorcerers and Glass Chewers — the Fire Eaters take Nourishment.

I

When an artist is so inspired by beauty that she must rise at six a.m. to paint before she catches a bus at one p.m., you may be sure there are going to be difficulties. At seven-thirty a.m. I had packed the Spirit with her stool, easel and paintbox into a white-canopied barouche and seen her clatter off in state behind two horses for the Garden of the Oudaias down by the Oued Bou Regreg, the River that Shines. Here she was to spend the morning at work, returning by twelve-fifteen p.m. to eat before we started for the Imperial city of Meknes ninety miles on.

At ten minutes to one the sun burned upon a solitary European figure that was myself, standing with a suitcase on the pavement outside the hotel. Round about this solitary figure, who from time to time pawed the ground impatiently as he searched the vistas of the streets in vain for some sign of the Spirit, a rabble of Arab boys pestered like flies, each determined to carry the suitcase.

And presently round a distant corner she comes scurrying like a trotting pony. Behind her a diminutive negro boy struggles along with easel and stool and paintbox. The allegiance of my Arab attendants is now divided. Some run off to intercept the small black boy and wrest the easel from his incompetent hands, whereupon ensues a fight which I prevent only by roaring out curses and "*imshis*" to the consternation of an elderly French lady emerging from the hotel.

" My watch stopped, I couldn't find a carriage, the picture's ruined, have we missed it ?" pants the Spirit.

"We have five minutes," I tell her. "Come on."

So with four Arab boys, having come into their own at last, carrying each a piece of luggage, and the remainder expressing their chagrin at defeat by doing their best to impede the successful ones, we set off down the Avenue Dar el Maghzen, which means the Avenue of the House of the Government, to the bus depot.

It lies at the bottom of the new town, on a broad avenue facing the rose-coloured walls of the old city. Here gather the buses that ply to and from all parts of North Morocco. They are none of your two-decker monsters, but of the charabanc type. Some are moderately comfortable though less spacious than those to which we are accustomed at home. Others are windowless and make no pretence of concealing the fact that they have seen their best days.

Some are crowded with Arabs swathed in white, Berbers in striped *djellabs*; others with a less colourful cargo of French men and women, with here and there the khaki and coloured braids of a military uniform. On top goes luggage of an infinite variety, ranging from elaborate blue and yellow suitcases to human beings and animals. From one bus bound for Casablanca a sheep peers over a bag of corn, bleating piteously down at us as though for help. On a second an unfortunate fowl, tied by its legs to the rail, eyes the world below with the resentful gaze of one with whom gross liberties are being taken.

We book our places at the bureau in the yard, while the bus is held up for us and the travellers within inspect our rabble of Arab attendants with their odd-looking baggage. " The Body" receives a suspicious poke from the conductor as it is un-ceremoniously slung on top of the bus. I drop a handful of small change among the attendants, where-upon another fight ensues as we scramble into our seats. We exchange a smile and a glance of satisfaction, for at last the vision of the grape-fruit has begun to be realised.

"Our first bus Sahara-wards," I say to the Spirit.

"Such a nice bus, too," she says. "Isn't it fun!"

And now we settle down, hungry but happy, to inspect our fellow travellers. There is but one Arab, a magnificent bearded man who keeps the hood of his mauve burnous over his head in spite of the heat. The rest are men and women in the dark drab clothes that civilisation imposes on us. They are not com-municative or friendly, these French colonials. They display no interest in each other or ourselves, but sit wrapped in a self-centred world of their own. In all the new French towns of Morocco we find them the same: the women bored, suspicious and unfriendly, with hard faces in which you will often see much that is spiteful and avaricious; the men indifferent and unresponsive to any friendly word or gesture. Now we are two people who laugh a good deal and can find enjoyment in life at its worst as well as at its best; and already we have found that our attitude is resented by the French here: it draws upon us many an unfriendly stare. Yet among the Arabs who are the conquered people, our freedom from care and readiness to smile is shared, as though we are more akin in spirit with them than with their conquerors . . .

Our bus speeds out of Rabat at a good forty miles an hour on a perfect road, and soon we are across the River that Shines, passing through a flat country of an unsurpassed fertility. Yellow cornfields ripple in the breeze, root crops grow to a gigantic size, olive trees twist themselves into fantastic shapes by the roadside. Sometimes we pass a village of mud-walled, straw-cone roofed huts, which look so picturesque outside with their stork guests perched on them but are so gloomy with poverty within.

Presently we round a bend in the road and approach something that appears to be a very smoky bonfire by the roadside. A great spiral of black smoke rises from some flaming mass. Around it at a safe distance, squatting in a circle, sit a score of Arab workers from the fields. At first we think we are about to witness some strange sacrificial rite, and the Spirit asks the driver if this is so.

" No, it's only a car," he says. " They *will* run into trees on this road after a little rain."

Hovering round the flaming car is its owner, helpless in the face of the fierce flames. The Arab audience has clearly settled down to enjoy the spectacle as an exciting diversion in the placidity of their lives. They are prepared to wait there for the rest of the day, so long as the car continues to burn. Our bus skirts the flames without stopping and speeds on, leaving the owner of the bonfire to whatever fate might befall him. At the village of Khemmiset, a place of white European bungalows beside a straw-roofed encampment, we pause to deliver mail and I am almost left behind in taking a stroll through the garden of an inn. Soon we pass among the green fertile hills and yellow rocks into the city of Meknes.

We pass the ancient city and travel on a mile to the new town, very white and clean and modern, reminding us of a chromium-plated snack bar. There are several bright, polished-looking cafés on the main street, their chairs of steel and red leather; and near the yard which is the bus depot we find a small white hotel which is no more than a double-fronted house behind a garden where lilies and oleanders grow.

As we enter the white tiled hall there is a flutter of wings and a rush of air past our faces, as half a dozen blue-backed swallows fly in and out. Round the roof of the hall, some ten feet above, they have their mud nests plastered in the angle of wall and ceiling. All day they flash in and out, feeding the young birds whose shrill demands are incessant till evening. The proprietor is an elderly Frenchman who tells us that the swallows come back every summer to their nests and bring luck to the house. He gives us a couple of white rooms with tiled floor for the equivalent of half-a-crown a day, and we are well pleased . . .

2

Now before we set out to explore this ancient Moorish city I want to give you a picture of the man who created it in its present form. He was that same Sultan Moulay Ismail who drove the English out of Tangier in 1684. They say he was a man short in stature, of tremendous virility, almost black — for his mother was a negro slave — with fierce bright eyes and an aquiline nose. He was one of the world's most enthusiastic builders. When he decided to make Meknes his capital, he pulled down most of the old town that stood here among the Zerhoun hills and determined to create another Versailles, which he had never seen. He went on building all his reign of fifty-five years. He even started to erect forty-foot high walls for 300 miles from Meknes to Marrakech to make a Royal highway for himself. His builders were some 30,000 slaves in chains, captured by the Barbary pirates from the coasts of Devon and Cornwall, France and Spain.

Ismail was a great warrior, treacherous, sensual, and evidently not averse from feminine charms, for he had 900 ladies who were wives and 3,000 who were not, which you will agree makes Solomon in all his glory look almost a misogynist. He had these ladies flogged if they failed to please him; who took a pomegranate from his garden without permission was put to death. There was also an English wife who could not appreciate the advantages of being converted to Islam, so, to make her see the light, he had her feet boiled in oil. Although he had more than 800 sons, it is clear that he believed in birth control, because most of his daughters were strangled at birth, often with his own hands. He attended personally to all the domestic affairs of his household, though you would think that among so many ladies he would have been able to find at least one good housekeeper.

Moulay Ismail had other hobbies besides building, marriage and strangling his daughters. One of them was killing people for the fun of it, and to keep up his prowess with spear and sword. Sometimes he would begin the day, after morning prayers, by riding out and spearing a dozen slaves who had been lined up for him. Often when he leapt into his saddle he would in the same movement cut off the head of the retainer who held the horse's bridle. And when he made rounds of inspection of his building operations, he would here and there slice off the head of a man who was not working hard enough and have his body built into the walls; for you must remember that there were no trade unions to raise objections to unorthodox building methods.

After he became Sultan he sent 10,000 heads of men, women and children to Fez and Marrakech, just to indicate that he meant business. Once he made a bridge of human bodies woven together with ropes to enable him to cross a river. He liked to feed his dog with flesh which he cut from a living woman; and the appetites of his menagerie of lions and tigers were always satisfied with live human beings. When his son and heir started a revolt which failed, Ismail cut off his right hand and foot, wept bitterly when the youth died, prayed for his sins, and built him a beautiful mausoleum. There is much more I could tell you of this incredible man, but I think this will be enough to justify the comment of an American to whom later I told something of Ismail's life. He said he guessed the guy must have been one of these here sadists. To which the only answer seems to be: You said it.

In one respect only can I find that Ismail resembled the English: he was kind to animals and had a passion for horses, of which he kept 4,000 each with its own personal groom and slave in attendance. When our own King Charles the Second gave Ismail three fine horses, the Sultan sent back a message that it was customary for horses to be in pairs, so would he kindly send him the fourth to match. I have been assured that his demand is still in the archives of Whitehall . . .

With the story of Moulay Ismail in our minds we walk the mile from the new town towards the fantastic city on the hill. Soon we are in the shadow of the vast ochre-coloured walls that tower 50 feet around the Imperial City. We emerge into the Place el Hedime, the great open square. You may guess what a spectacle it was when I tell you that the Spirit almost wept because she had not brought her painting apparatus. She wanted to sit there and then to transfer to her canvas some of the fantastic life and colour that surged around us.

The great open space amid the walls is thronged with a diversity of humanity, with small tents and stalls, with negroes in rags, Moors in spotless white, Berbers in striped *djellabs*, Sudanese from the far south, veiled women. There are faces jet black, faces brown and fierce, pale parchment-coloured faces that mark the aristocratic Moor. There is a surge of life and a babel of talk in this sunny square, where life has gone on unchanged since the days when Ismail held sway.

We are hailed by a water-seller, a tall negro with a cheerful grin, who walks among the crowd jangling his brass bell. His water, drawn from one of the city fountains, is in a goatskin bag slung under his arm. He wears white shorts and a red tunic which is adorned with many shining silver ornaments and coins; two dazzlingly polished cups dangle in front of him. He holds one of them out at arms length, presses the bag with his elbow and with unerring aim syphons into the cup a jet of ice-cold water, for which he charges a fraction of a farthing. We do not drink, for safety's sake, but ask him to pose for a photograph; whereupon he makes a great display of his skill, squirting a jet into his own mouth, into the mouth of an acquaintance six feet away, then into the ear of a passing Arab boy, whose shrill protests raise a gust of merriment among the bystanders. The water-seller is proud of his sureness of aim and his polished cups and red tunic. We meet many of his kind in the towns of Morocco, wandering in the crowds and through the streets, ringing their bells as a hint that nobody need go thirsty.

A white-robed snake charmer sitting in the dust calls out to us, eager to perform for a franc or two; but we pass into the labyrinthine ways of the market of tents, where a thousand and one traders offer their wares spread on cloths on the ground. There are fruits and vegetables and meat, expanses of sweet-smelling mint for the tea-making, white cones of sugar, herbs and spices, cinnamon and lavender and rose petals, grain in small heaps over which fierce-eyed Berbers meditate and argue.

Then there is the native doctor, who claims to cure

not only your bodily but also your spiritual ailments. He drives out evil spirits. Turbaned and bearded he sits before an array of herbs and powders of all colours, laid out in small bags. Around him are a multitude of other strange objects — hares' feet, horns and pelts of animals, snake skins, pieces of bark, rats' skulls — all of which he uses to charm away your ills. An eagle chained by the leg sits beside him, to heighten the dramatic effects of his performances.

A young Berber crouches beside the doctor, taking a cure. He opens his hand to receive a small quantity of green powder, and while the doctor sprinkles it into his palm he murmurs an incantation. Then he takes up a bone and rubs on the young man's forehead, still muttering some magical formula. For this cure the young man pays him a few centimes and goes off satisfied.

A small Arab boy with a gentle ingenuous face attached himself to us and trots at our side, murmuring little explanations of everything in which we take interest. Like all the children and young people in Morocco, he speaks fluent though ungrammatical French; it is only the very old men, who were set in their ways before the French occupation, whose talk is confined to their own language.

We pass now to the Bab el Mansour, the great gateway that opens into the Imperial City. And here we begin to feel the influence of Moulay Ismail, with this first impression of his stupendous building projects. For this is not so much a gate as a cathedral. Its massive carved bastions and Moorish archways are supported by marble columns taken from the Roman city of Volubilis, relic of Rome's African Empire of more than 2,000 years ago, whose ruins lie a few miles away. Its interior is so immense that some 500 people can find shelter. Blind beggars in rags crouch against the walls in the twilight of the interior, chanting their

monotonous pleas for alms for the love of Allah.
Hands stretch out of the dimness and clutch in appeal
at our feet and legs as we pass through to the sunlight
beyond.

And here, in the Imperial City itself, Moulay Ismail
envelops and overpowers us. His vast walls imprison
us. For miles they tower beside the wide dusty roads,
forming rose-tinted corridors through which a surge
of native life incessantly passes. But much of their
original magnificence is lost, for they were built too
speedily for permanence; like many of the palaces of
this fantastic ruler, they are falling into decay. There
are crumbling holes in them, which the Spirit suggests
were the tombs of the unhappy slaves whom Ismail
built into these vast structures. It is a grim thought
to realise that these walls in places are lined with
skeletons, many of them the remains of tragic Englishmen who fell into the hands of the Monster of Meknes.

Our small Arab attachment, who tells us his name
is Moktar, points to a high, plain building with a great
arched doorway and a pointed roof of green tiles, and
with awe in his voice says: "*La tombe de Moulay
Ismail.*" It seems that even to this day the Bloody
Sultan's name strikes fear to the descendants of his
subjects. We are not permitted to enter the sacred
building, but we peer through the arched doorway
into an outer chamber whose floor is of earth and
whose walls, like all things in Meknes, are falling to
decay. The tomb of the tyrant is not visible to the
curious eyes of Unbelievers. It is a holy place, as you
can tell from the green tiles of the roof, which are
given only to tombs and mosques; for green was the
colour of the turban of Mahomet.

Through another great gateway in a mile-long
corridor of road and walls we pass the entrance to the
Palace, a vast carved doorway in the wall. But here
again entrance is forbidden: black sentries stand on

guard. So we sit for a while by the road at the foot of the towering wall and meditate on Moulay Ismail, trying to picture the scenes of magnificence and terror that once were witnessed in this great corridor of a road. Moktar sits cross-legged beside us, his chin in his hand, watching us with his shy eyes and listening to our incomprehensible talk with a little smile. He is unlike most of the Arab boys who haunt the cities: he does not pester, but is content to trot beside us when we walk, to sit with us as long as we care to sit, and to answer any questions we ask.

When we rise to return Moktar murmurs: " *Vous voudrai voir les autruches ?*"

"Ostriches?" the Spirit exclaims in surprise. " Where are the ostriches?"

He leads us along the interminable road to the end of the walls, through a gate and along the edge of a field to an enclosure among trees. Here a dozen of the ridiculous birds strut about in a desultory manner, staring down at us with protuberant goggle eyes. Moktar gurgles with laughter as he watches the slow, rhythmic plod of their great feet.

" *Comme un chameau*," he said; which was an excellent simile.

We are joined by a negro boy who seemed to be jealous of Moktar's friendship with us; perhaps, too, he wants to share in any *pourboire* that may be dispensed later. He supplements Moktar's comments with scraps of information from his own store. The pair of them walk on either side of us as we continue our wandering.

Presently we come to a blank-faced, pale rose-coloured building which proves to be one of the store-houses for Ismail's grain. It is doorless now, so we enter and find ourselves in the darkness of a vast cavern. One or two dimly-seen greyish figures stir in the gloom. We exit hurriedly. Moktar says the place is used now by homeless wanderers who have no place to live.

Ahead of us is the lake of Sahridj Souani, which Ismail built for his pleasure. Sometimes he sailed on it in a luxurious boat with his women, sometimes he would drown a few people in its waters for the fun of watching their last struggles. If a wife on board displeased him, he dropped her overboard. The lake has no beauty now; it is no more than a large muddy pond with broken banks. Moktar says you must not come here at night, because an evil *djinn* haunts the place. The negro says it once chased him for many kilometres. I ask them what this particular *djinn* is like, but neither can tell, they know only that it is a very terrible *djinn*.

We are out of the city now, on the edge of the country, and the roads are deserted except for a pair of laden camels moving slowly towards us in charge of an Arab. We are tired, and are regretting that we have several miles to walk on the return journey.

"I wish to heaven we could ride," said the Spirit, slipping off a shoe and tenderly caressing her toes.

Now I do not know whether a caress to ones toes has the effect, similar to the rubbing of a magic lamp, of propitiating the genii that has power to make one's wishes come true. But at that same moment there was a clatter of hoofs, and a rickety barouche, driven by an ancient Arab, came round a distant corner on its way to the city.

We climbed in after I had given Moktar and his negro a few francs each, and the carriage had started when our attention was drawn by a scuffle and a cry from behind. We looked round and saw little Moktar engaged in what seemed to be mortal combat with the negro.

"*Voleur, voleur*," cried Moktar, "he tries to steal my francs."

In a second the Spirit was out of the carriage, belabouring the thick black negro head with the handle of my stick. The owner of the head cried out in a loud voice and fled. Moktar stammered his thanks, his shy eyes glowing with gratitude.

"For that," said the Spirit, "you shall ride back with us. I'll have none of this highway robbery, not even in Ismail's city."

I think Moktar was the proudest small boy in Meknes that evening, as he rolled back to town in the seat opposite ourselves. He said he had never ridden before in a carriage with a white sun awning. When we came back to the crowded places he leaned well forward, seeking to show himself to any acquaintances who might pass. And when we put him down near the Bab el Mansour he stood watching until we disappeared round an angle of the great wall.

3

There is a muffled throbbing of many drums this evening in the great open space beside the Bab el Mansour just inside the walls of the Imperial City. They have an insistence that draws us irresistibly and an urgency that speeds our steps. Their rapid rhythms blend in a rumble of sound that pervades the city and obsesses our minds so that we must answer their summons.

This drumming we hear is the Call of the Entertainers, for it is the feast day of one of Islam's many local saints and the crowds have come to town to celebrate with song and story, dance and music. We pass with the multitude through the great gateway into the open space which is the theatre of Meknes; and at once we are enveloped in a whirlpool of coloured humanity. Audiences stand and sit around a variety of entertainers in groups large or small, according to the drawing power of the artists. Beside each entertainer is an assistant who beats a drum, which is no more than a large pottery vase with a skin stretched across in place of a pottery base. The drummer holds the instrument under his arm and beats alternately with palm and finger-tips, calling to the multitude to witness the miracles his master is to perform. Each has a different rhythm, each beats out a variation of the eternal hollow *tunk-a-tunk-tunk* which all over Africa has its meaning for those who can understand.

In this place of entertainment there is a joyous savagery which well suits the city of Moulay Ismail. In the variegated crowds are faces wild, dark and cruel from the far south, with gleaming eyes avid for excitement. There are negroid faces with aquiline noses and fierce eyes that make us wonder if they may not be descendants of some of the many sons of Ismail. There are cripples pleading plaintively for alms, and four blind men in rags, each with a hand on the other's shoulder, passing slowly through the throng chanting prayers. Three veiled women sit in a group singing a plaintive Arab song. And over all is the persuasive *tunk-tunk* of the drums, speeding the pulses, drawing the ear and eye.

Here is the snake charmer. His long black hair hangs Medusa-like from a yellow turban round his dark face, his eyes glitter wildly, his movements are spectacularly dramatic. The rapt crowd squats and stands around him, leaving a circle of earth for his stage. A small boy beside him monotonously beats the drum, while the charmer makes elaborate preparations by running his hands through his hair, declaiming in a loud, rapid voice as he crouches before a small covered barrel. He is working up the interest, piling up the curiosity; he has all the tricks of the cheapjack salesman of our English markets. He knows well how to hold the attention while he awaits a larger audience.

And when at last he uncovers the barrel and the entertainment begins, he still must keep up the excitement, for the snakes give him little assistance. These two ugly black cobras seem to be very lethargic and bored snakes : they would so clearly prefer to stay in their barrel. He twirls them round his neck, uttering the while many a savage cry; he makes one of them bite on his arm, drawing blood; then with many dramatic preparations he thrusts the sinister black head into his mouth, his face grimacing horribly. The snake emerges flickering its forked tongue; the charmer works himself into a frenzy as he throws the reptile around his body; the crowd applauds. Only the snake was unimpressed by his daring.

Despite his frenzy, the charmer has not failed to observe our presence, for we are the only Europeans in this tempestuous crowd. He rises now and comes to us, his snakes hanging round his neck, flickering their tongues. The Spirit shrinks back, but he takes her hand and bends over it, rubbing it with an end of his long shaggy hair.

" *Porte bonheur*," he cried. " *Porte bonheur*."

It costs me a franc, that piece of good luck.

We turn aside to another entertainer, feeling a little sorry for him because he has an audience of only four small boys. He is a very old, white-bearded man, and he twangs a battered two-string lute as he dances lumberingly on a pile of broken glass with his naked feet. Yet he seems not to suffer from this odd method of entertainment, perhaps because his feet are leathered through barefoot walking on burning sands. Sometimes he makes a quavering piping sound that is intended to be a song.

Next to him, with a larger audience, is an aged man chewing glass. He fills his mouth full of small pieces and goes through an elaborate and excruciating pantomime of eating and enjoying it; and presently he shoots it out in little glittering showers on to a cloth spread on the ground. The crowd tosses a few centimes into the cloth and passes on.

And here are four mournful half-negroes from the south, sitting in a circle in the yellow dust, swaying towards each other and back again as they chant a monotonous shrill wailing song of one line, endlessly repeated. One beats a pottery drum, another twangs a guenbri, the small Moroccan three-stringed mandolin carved from a tree's bough. They seem to have doped themselves with the incessance of their short song, for their eyes are glazed and unseeing, and the sway of their bodies is like the movement of tired men who are falling asleep.

And now from a larger group emerges the small figure of Moktar, smiling a shy greeting and making a way for us to enter the circle. The eyes of this crowd are concentrated on a tall bearded Arab in white, who stands declaim-like some prophet of old, so great is his dignity, so impressive his manner. In the East the story-teller is still the main source of the people's entertainment. He is to the Arab what the novel and the film are to the European: for those who cannot read must yet have their romances. This teller of tales is well versed in the dramatic, he is an actor as well as an orator. With gestures sometimes slow and deliberate, sometimes wild and abandoned, he tells some strange fantasy in flowing, flowery Arabic, while the crowd stands rapt in the convolutions of his tale. Their mouths gape open and the eyes in their brown and black faces react to every gesture: sometimes wide and shining with excitement, then turning sombre as the tale takes a new turn, and again gleaming as some humour draws their full-throated laughter. They wander from city to city, these story-tellers, from far south to the north, giving their ancient romances to the people. Sometimes they tell tales that were first told by Scheherazade in the Arabian Nights; or else they speak of the saints and their miracles, or of the heroic adventures of long-dead sultans.

We ask Moktar what is this romance we are now hearing but cannot understand, and he gives us an outline of it.

It is a simple tale, with a moral that fosters the Islamic subjection of women. There was a certain rich man who had a very lovely wife; so lovely was she that when she emerged into the garden of her husband the sun veiled himself and the jasmine flowers closed because they were ashamed of their ugliness. Now this wife appears to have been a bit of a termagant who traded on her beauty. Whenever her husband went on a journey she instructed him to buy her this and that — a robe of silk, a caftan of gold and silver and rare jewels; and so uxorious was the fellow that he obeyed her every whim. Yet she was never satisfied, but always wanted more; until at last the husband had so little money that he was no longer able to defend his lands, and an enemy came and fought him and took all his possessions, giving the beautiful wife to his vizier for a slave.

Then the unhappy husband was brought before the conqueror, who heard his tale and spoke thus: "Give him a caftan of finest silk and place a veil over his face and put him in my harem. Only a woman can obey a woman, so that this creature is no man; he will look well in my harem."

The crowd are delighted with the tale. They laugh gleefully at the fate of the rich man, considering it to be well-deserved; for they know that no true follower of the Prophet could suffer dictation by a woman.

Through the crowds we reach the sorcerer, an aged

black man sitting in a charmed circle drawn in the dust. Within the circle are some old earthen bottles which Moktar says are love philtres and charms. A veiled woman sits before the man, telling him her troubles in a low voice from beneath her yashmak. Moktar strays near to listen, then tells us that the woman's husband has taken to himself another and younger wife and that she fears to lose his love.

The old sorcerer produces a stub of red chalk, writes some mystic symbols on a scrap of paper, and passes it to her with a muttered incantation. She slips it beneath her white robes and steals unobtrusively away to be lost in the crowd, perhaps with new hope in a heart that was heavy with woe.

And now we are drawn by a clamour of hoarse cries, towards which Moktar hurries us, his eyes big with excitement.

"*Ils mangent le feu*," he says. "*C'est terrible*."

Here in the greatest crowd of all are five wild, half-naked men, lashing themselves into a frenzy as they gyrate round a fire on the ground. They are the fire-eaters of the Aissaoua, fanatical followers of a religious sect founded by Sidi Mahomed ben Aissa, saint of Meknes whose tomb lies in another part of the city. Their long hair, sign of the dervish, the mystic and the holy men, flows behind them as they circle the fire, drawing from it flaming torches which they thrust into their howling mouths and beat upon their naked chests. Suddenly one of the dervishes, clothed only in a loin-cloth, hurls himself down beside the fire and rolls over it and back again; leaps up calling wildly on Allah and his saint, seizes another torch from the fire and beats it upon his back as he whirls round again in the circle. The wild dark faces of the crowd watch with a horrid fascination in their eyes. Sometimes one of them, carried away by the frenzy, himself breaks into a wild cry of exaltation.

Moktar himself is panting with excitement, trembling with some ecstatic emotion which we cannot feel because the minds and the ways of the fanatical East are beyond our understanding.

Presently, when we are moving through another part of this place of entertainment, we find these fire-eaters resting beside the towering wall. The frenzy has gone from them now, they are calm and very friendly. The Spirit pauses to examine the torches which lie beside them, and a tall gaunt Berber, who a while before had been screaming like a maniac as he rolled in fire, tentatively hands one for her inspection. There is no madness in his face now, only a gentle almost shy expression; about all these five men we discern a calmness of spirit, as though the savagery had been burnt out of them. The torch is a bar of wood bound tightly round at one end with paper dipped in tallow. The fire-eater speaks something incomprehensible to the Spirit in a Berber dialect we do not understand, and his voice is no more than a hoarse whisper: it seems that his art had almost deprived him of the power of speech.

" Ask him if it is painful, this eating of fire," the Spirit tells Moktar, who puts the question to the performer.

The fire-eater shakes his head and with a saintly smile answers at some length.

" He says it is not painful," says Moktar. " He says the saints protect him from fire, and that Allah the All Merciful gives him power to do what other men may not do."

Thereupon the fire-eater turned to one of his confreres who had rolled naked on the flames and uncovered the man's back. The Spirit examined him with care, but found no sign of burns. We wonder by what strange trickery a man is able to roll on fire and come to no harm; for we are no believers in the power of dead saints to protect living flesh from the elements.

Then the fire-eater produces a box of matches and lights the tallowed end of his torch. He waves it in the air and for our special benefit thrusts it into his mouth, putting out the flames. Happily he does not again go into a frenzy.

"No wonder the poor man has laryngitis," said the Spirit, as I give the gentle creature a franc.

Moktar tells us there are to be some strange goings-on at the Bab Berdayne, one of the gates on the far side of the city. Near here lies the tomb of Aissa, where the passion of the Aissaoua reaches its climax.

As we approach we hear strange wild cries and wailings, and presently we come upon a sight that might have been inspired by bloodthirsty Moulay Ismail himself.

A crowd of wildly dancing men are surging down towards the saint's tomb, preceded by several horsemen. Some are in rags, some in bright colours, some half naked. They dance with the frenzy of fanatics, whirling like dervishes, darting forward and backward. Blood streams from self-inflicted wounds on their faces and bodies. Some of them clasp thorny branches to themselves, tearing their flesh. One dark madman with streaming hair claps the flat pads of a prickly cactus to his chest, throws himself rolling on the ground in his ecstasy, so that the yellow dust mingles with his blood into a crimson paste which plasters him until he is scarcely recognisable. Thus the crowd of fanatics pass on towards the tomb to worship . . .

We escape from the imprisoning crowd and seek a quiet place beside the wall where we can avoid the dust-cloud which these whirling holy men have raised.

Now it may be some trick of the imagination, but

it seems to me that in the twilight I detect a peculiar expression in the Spirit's eyes.

"We'd better find some food," I said.

She nods.

"After that," she says tensely, "I want a bloody steak and some red wine."

I fear the spirit of Moulay Ismail is entering into her. Perhaps we shall need the services of the sorcerer after all.

4

The fanaticism of Meknes produces a reaction which impels us to seek less bloodthirsty entertainment. The underdone steak which appeased the Spirit's hunger seemed also to have exorcised the *djinn* which I feared was taking possession of her; and in the morning she was prepared for adventure of a more peaceful kind. She had enjoyed, she said, a surfeit of blood and fire, but suggested now the advisability of an archaeological excursion, since one cannot get blood from stones. It was agreed, then, that we should set off to explore the ruins of Volubilis, chief town of Mauretania Tingitania, which was the African Empire of ancient Rome.

It lies some twenty miles from Meknes and can be reached only by car. So at ten o'clock the universal provider who is our host at the House of the Swallows brings to his door a taxicab which will take us not only to Volubilis but to Moulay Idris, the holy city, for fifty francs.

The day is sunny but cold, for Meknes stands high among the fertile hills. Soon we are out among them, passing over roads that run like smooth switchbacks through cultivated fields and olive groves which already give the country an Italian air. Sometimes we pass a Berber or two, driving a burdened donkey or working on the land; sometimes the inevitable camel looks up disdainfully from his browsing. There is peace here amid the solitude of the Zerhoun hills, through which once the Roman legions marched on their way to new conquests.

We stop at a small white house and are met by three or four shy Berber children who offer bunches of flowers for anything we like to give in exchange. There is really no need to buy, for all around us now grow masses of deep blue anchusa, to be had for the plucking; but the Spirit can never resist the charm of a floral greeting, so we buy while we are being greeted by a young Berber, who acts as guide to the long-dead city.

Over muddy tracks where once Roman chariots drove we climb to the hill of Volubilis, wandering through streets that are silent now except for the sighing of the wind in the grass and the soft voice of the young Berber, who in fluent French tells us the secrets of this long-dead city. It has not the completeness of Pompeii or Herculaneum, but possesses most of the attributes that we have found in every Roman city we have visited. There is, for example, the House of the Dog, as in Pompeii, though here the dog is a metal one, housed now in the small museum near the entrance. Our young Berber shows us the vestiges of the forum with its broken pillars; he leads us over fine mosaic floors, into stone wine-presses with their channels that carried away the grape-juice to the vats of the wine-seller. He is proud of the relics of the drainage system, stone channels that run under the ground, and of the rich man's house with its central heating system and bathing pool; but he tactfully ignores the very phallic symbols carved over the doorway, fearing perhaps to embarrass us.

He takes pride too, in interpreting the meaning of the mosaics and explaining how the great triumphal arch which dominates the city was built in AD 217 to commemorate the victories of Caracalla.

As in all such relics of dead empires, there is a brooding melancholy in Volubilis, where once some sixteen thousand Romans loved and sorrowed and hoped. Before them on this spot were the Carthaginians; after them the Vandals, slaying and destroying; and as a final blow to the once prosperous city came Moulay Ismail, tearing down its marble columns to build his gates and palaces. Now it is given over to the winds and the rain; and lizards flash among its baths and wine-presses like streaks of emerald lightning; and wandering travellers like ourselves eat sandwiches and drink red wine under the broken arch that tells of Caracalla's triumphs, so worthy of commemoration then, so unimportant now.

We say farewell to our Berber guide, after asking him how much he wants for his services. He shrugs and says whatever we will, so I give him ten francs, knowing it is excessive. Yet when a man trusts to one's conscience, he impels one to be generous; only when he haggles and argues does he rouse one's instinct to be mean.

Soon we are switchbacking again over the mountain roads, circling and climbing until we come in sight of Moulay Idris, a white town mounting to the spur of a green hill. It is the oldest Moslem city in Morocco. Until a few years ago no unbeliever was permitted to tread its holy ground. Even to-day only the Faithful may own property or live within its walls; and its inhabitants pay no taxes to the State.

It was here that Moulay Idris founded the first Arab dynasty in Morocco when he fled from his enemies. He was a descendant of Fatima, daughter of Mahomet. The eighth century found him in Volubilis, preaching the faith to the Berber tribes who then inhabited that relic of the might of Rome. He became their ruler and founded for them this city on the mountain, where now his saintly body lies under a green-roofed tomb so holy that only the Sultan may enter the presence.

A final twist in the mountain road brings us through an arched gateway in the town wall into an open space amid Moorish shops and houses, where we alight. The Spirit irreverently remarks that if cleanliness is next to godliness, Allah must be a long way from Moulay Idris. There has been a shower of rain, and we squelch through deep yellow mud that sucks at our heels like quicksand, avoiding small heaps of garbage which have been thrown from shops and houses. "You would think," says she, "that they might make the approach to the holiest spot in all Morocco a little less unpleasant."

Guided by a young man in a dirty *djellab* and greasy fez, we cross the open space to a passage that leads to the tomb. It is lined with small shops where men pester us to buy holy candles and other relics at exorbitant prices. Half way along the passage our way is barred by a massive wooden turnpike, beyond which as Christians we must not pass. So we stand and gaze at the entrance to the white-walled, green-tiled building at the end, watching Moors enter to pray with that sense of frustration we always feel when excluded from something which others are permitted to enjoy.

Inside the door of the tomb is a great alms chest into which the Faithful deposit gifts which go to the descendants of the holy Idris. There are many of them in this city; our guide tells us that they make much money, very much money. As descendants of the Prophet through Idris they are holy men, ranking as *Sharifs*. It is a good thing in Morocco to be able to claim so exalted a pedigree, for you need then have no anxiety about earning a living. A *Sharif* will never want for sustenance or shelter. Doubtless that is one reason why there are so many *Sharifs* in the country; though I have been told that the pedigrees of many would not bear even a superficial investigation.

We buy for two francs a ten-centime candle while our guide tells us how bad are the times now in Moulay Idris. There is no great pilgrimage this year, because everybody is so poor and cannot afford to come. He is grateful for the three francs I give him, and closes the car door on us with a fine flourish and a farewell wave of his hand. And as we swing out into the winding road for the descent, the Spirit sums up her impressions of the day.

"Volubilis is lovely and tragic," she says, "but Moulay Idris is too consciously and uncleanly holy for me. Let's get back to the city of blood and fire". . .

That night we dined in a small and friendly French restaurant which we found in one of the side streets of Meknes. The *crème St. Germain* was good; the *omelette aux fines herbes* was excellent; the roast fowl was tender though a little burnt; the oranges and figs the best that Morocco produces, which means that they were very good indeed. Wine was strong, unlimited and free; it is as plentiful in this country as in France, and they make no charge for it at meals. From the wineshops we can buy a good bottle of *rouge, rosé* or *blanc* for three francs, or fourpence halfpenny. It is a pleasure to drink if only for the fascination of its labels. My favourite here is Beni Amer, which takes its name from the village where it is made a few miles from Meknes. Then there is good strong red Meknassi, golden or rosé Sidi Larbi, and a positively head-reeling Beni Snassen for six or seven francs the bottle.

Our meal cost four shillings and sixpence for the two; and we went to bed that night well fortified for the next stage of the journey by bus.

CHAPTER 5.

Tells of the Valley of Nightingales — City of Secrets — the Trap of the Sharif — Fanaticism — School for Hatred — Flowery Invitation — Hassan Pays a Call — a Feast with Youssef ben Tayyib — Love Song — Vices and Sorceries — the House of the Dancing Perverts — Card Games in Arcady.

I

Our bus for Fez, the next stopping place in our journey, left at two o'clock in the afternoon; so that we had a morning to spare for wandering in Meknes. The Spirit was up at six o'clock, and at eight was keeping an appointment with Moktar at the shop of his father. Moktar had promised to sit for his portrait. To-day was to be a great event in his life.

The small shop, where the elderly solemn parent sat sewing amid an assortment of silks and satins and braids for the adornment of feminine beauty, stood in the shadow of a mosque in the *medina*, the native town. Moktar was eager for his new experience, but his father was not whole-hearted in his approval. You must know that the creation of graven images, whether in stone or in portraiture, was forbidden by Mahomet and is contrary to the strict interpretation of the laws of Islam. Mahomet's decree served its purpose, which was to discourage the worship of a multitude of gods and confine it to the one true God; but it checked the development of pictorial art among Moslems, so that the Arab genius for ever afterwards has expressed itself in architecture instead of in paint. To many of the simpler Moors there is danger in this reproduction of the human form; it brings ill luck to the subject of the portrait and places him in the power of the painter, who henceforth may be able to inflict evil upon him. When you try to photograph an Arab, the chances are that he will turn aside, or conceal his face, or grow angry, as did an old man on whom my camera was directed in the town. Or he will raise the fingers of one hand between you and himself to ward off the evil eye.

But Moktar cares for none of these superstitions. He pleads with his father, and at last the old man assents, allowing Moktar to sit cross-legged among the silks and girdles while the Spirit goes about this magic business of painting him.

Soon the narrow alley of a street in which she sits is impassable because of the crowd that gathers. Arabs and veiled women stand around her ten deep, watching every stroke of the brush. The sight of these bright colours emerging from their tubes delights them. At each squeeze of a new tube they wait breathlessly until they see the bright colour, then exhale their breath in little "ah-h-hs" of satisfaction. Moktar is inordinately proud of himself; for the first time in his life he is the centre of a crowd's interest. He is a perfect model, for despite his youth he has all the resignation and calm of the Oriental.

When the picture is finished he comes back with us to the House of the Swallows and insists on carrying "The Body" to the bus. He sees to it that we are comfortable; and as we glide away his eyes rest longingly on the case that contains the magic coloured representation of himself.

The journey of forty miles is uneventful. Our fellow passengers are the usual French colonials, with a sprinkling of uniformed officers and soldiers and a few Moors. The country through which we pass varies little from that which circles Meknes. Within two hours we are in the new French town of Fez, bright and polished and dazzling like all French-Moroccan creations.

We had been recommended to an hotel on the edge of the ancient native city of Fez, but when we inquire the way at the bus depot we find we are a good two miles from it. So we hire the ubiquitous barouche with its two decrepit horses and ragged Arab driver. He takes us clattering and rambling round dusty roads beside high walls, up hills and through valleys, until we are deposited on a hillside beside a white house whose wide balconies hang over a valley that shines silver-green with olive groves in the setting sun.

An Arab boy takes our luggage, a business-like Frenchwoman shows us rooms, and in ten minutes we are sitting on our balcony over a cup of tea. And when the sunlight has left the valley and the crimson clouds beyond the darkening hills are fading to pale gold, the song of a nightingale rises from below. Like a sudden paean for the ancient glories of Fez it comes to us out of the silence. Soon it is answered by the song of another nightingale from a tree not twenty yards away; and by the time night has fallen a dozen, a score are singing in the valley, sending up a symphony whose ecstasy seems to draw the stars earthward to listen. We sit enchanted, unable to tear ourselves away from this Valley of the Nightingales; and when at last we go down to the barren restaurant and comment on this loveliness to madame, she shrugs indifferently and says: "*Ah, oui, c'est toujours comme ça*," as she continues to write out the menu.

2

We have an introduction to a certain *caid*, or tribal ruler, in this city of Fez, and before we set out to explore in the morning we send him by negro messenger a letter which informs him of our arrival. In the meantime we decide to see as much of Fez as we can, so that when we meet we shall not be entirely ignorant of his city.

But we have undertaken a task greater than we realise. This ancient city created eleven hundred years ago by Moulay Idris the Second, son of the founder of the first dynasty, is the largest and most complicated in Morocco. At first we walk interminably on the white road that circles it, between high blank yellow walls, to the accompaniment of the pestilential chatter of three Arab youths who have attached themselves to us, determined to act as guides. Presently we come to a small door in the wall, pass through, and in a moment we are swallowed up, lost, in Fez the Mysterious, the teeming, exotic city that hides itself from the sun. It is as though we had stepped suddenly from reality into some fantasy of the days of Haroun al Raschid.

We are in a labyrinth of alleys where men move mysteriously in twilight amid the poverty and dirt and gorgeous trappings of the East; alleys lined with cavernous shops in which men sit silently at work at their arts and crafts, surrounded by the brilliant coloured wares of Morocco. Above, the streets are roofed with a lattice of canes into which rushes are woven, so that the sunlight comes through in fine narrow bars which make strange flickering mysteries of the people who pass below. All sound is subdued, all bright light is withheld, so that a strangely sinister air pervades the city. On and on the narrow dim streets wind and cross, sometimes emerging into wider spaces where fountains, exquisitely tiled, splash cascades at which veiled women gather to fill their water jars; sometimes plunging into utter darkness under the foundations of an unseen palace, to emerge again into a bazaar where laden donkeys and mules edge through the throngs to warning cries of "*Balek*" from their owners. We pass a narrow doorway in a high blank wall and glimpse beyond some sunlit court where fountains play amid trees heavy with oranges and citrons and nectarines. Or we look through an archway that gives glimpses of the great hall of some *medersa* or college, where aged men who have spent their lives in the study of philosophy and law sit beside quiet pools under walls carved with the exquisite lace-like traceries and fretworks of ancient Moorish art. In this centre of learning and commerce, this spiritual headquarters of the Moors, there is no outward display of fine architecture: it is hidden behind high walls and approached by these tortuous streets that teem with the poverty and colour of Africa.

We know we are lost, but we do not care. We wander on, through the Street of the Marriage Belts, where men sit in their open shops creating gorgeous bands of purple and gold and silver embroidery for the adornment of brides; through the Street of the Shoemakers, the Souk of the Clockmakers, the Street of Carpenters. Each trade is segregated and has a special region of its own; and each is controlled by a mediaeval Guild such as we had in England in the days long past. We pause at the sound of rushing water, and see a stream frothing and bubbling through the half-light: there are scores of these rivulets, diverted from the main river that runs through Fez to supply the fountains and gardens of the city.

Watchful eyes from the shops follow us as we pass, but we are not asked to buy. There is an aloofness about the people of Fez which adds to the mysteriousness of their city. They do not welcome strangers who are Christians. We are surprised, then, when we are passing through one of the *souks*, to receive a hearty greeting from a magnificent Moor who approaches with a group of four retainers at his heels. He is evidently a man of substance, even of importance. He is splendidly robed in white and has a full black beard and dark shining eyes from which his welcome glows. He stops and shakes hands, saying we are welcome to Fez. He asks in French whence we came and where we are staying, and adds that he has many English friends. Will we do him the honour of visiting his house and signing his guest book, in which we may find the names of many of his friends? His manner is so courteous, his eagerness to be friendly so marked, that we cannot but accept. He tells us his name, and we note that he is a *Sharif*. We are actually speaking to a descendant of the Prophet. We feel that this is indeed a worth-while encounter.

The *Sharif* turns to one of his retainers to instruct him, then tells us: "My servant will take you to my house and you will have refreshment. I ask pardon that I cannot join you now, for I am upon a mission; but we shall meet again when you are refreshed."

With a graceful gesture he passed on, while we followed his servant, a slim young Moor.

"The *Sharif* is a distinguished man in Fez?" the Spirit asks him.

"He is one of the great men of Fez," the youth replies. "He is rich and owns many palaces and many wives. Madame shall visit his harem if she wishes."

We come soon to a doorway and pass through into a great Moorish courtyard, tiled in purple and white. It is open to the sky on one side; on the other are divans and small low carved tables of cedarwood. A wide marble stair climbs to the rooms above. There is a delicate perfume of jasmine in the air.

We sit on a divan, and while the retainer orders mint tea and almond pastries to be set before us, we study the famous guest book. There are indeed many names, some of them appended to flattering remarks on the hospitality of the *Sharif*: it is evident that these people have appreciated his friendliness. There are snapshots of the *Sharif* sitting in his court with Europeans, standing at his door receiving them. It is very evident that the *Sharif* is one of the hospitable men of Fez.

When we are refreshed, the retainer asks the Spirit if she would care to visit the harem. He calls out in a loud voice, and a negress dressed in crimson and white emerges from nowhere and escorts her up the staircase. I remain behind, for it is not permitted that men shall invade the sanctity of the women's quarters. The retainer sits on the tiled floor, dreamily twanging a lute while I dawdle over my mint tea, enjoying the peace and loveliness of this court. A white dove flutters down to drink at a fountain which splashes from a blue-tiled recess in the wall.

When the Spirit returns she is a little disappointed.

"Not a very exciting harem," she says. "Two elderly and rather sullen women sitting on cushions doing embroidery. The negress says the other ladies of the harem are away at one of his other palaces."

The retainer puts down his lute.

"The *Sharif* wishes that you shall meet him again at his other house," he says. "It is very wonderful, and full of his splendid treasures. It is not far, now that you are refreshed."

He is such a gentle, soft-spoken retainer that we feel we would follow him anywhere. He takes us again through the labyrinthine streets, where the halt and the maimed and the blind sit crying for alms in the dust beside the secretive doorways of *medersas* and hidden mosques.

Presently we are ushered through a narrow door-way.

And beyond that doorway the truth comes to us.

Disillusionment falls upon us.

Disillusionment, and the *Sharif*, and three retainers.

"Good heavens, it's a ramp," exclaims the Spirit.

We are in a shop, and the *Sharif's* splendid treasures are indeed all around us. From floor to ceiling of the small room they are piled: Moorish leather goods of every kind and shape; handbags, purses, bookmarks, pouffe covers and a multitude of other goods, all factory made and of the poorest material. On the wall a notice in French states that this is the only shop in Fez where prices are honestly and clearly marked on the goods, so that there need be no argument. And what prices they are!

The *Sharif* is courteous as ever, but there is a new firmness about him, a determination and a powerful persuasiveness. As he presses upon us this and that article marked at an exorbitant price, he asks with the eagerness of one whose sole aim in life is to please whether we have enjoyed his entertainment. His retainers hem us in so that there is no escape; and they, too, press into our hands his splendid treasures. A leather bag which we could buy elsewhere for twenty francs costs sixty here; a small Arab purse worth four francs is twenty.

Now in the past we have encountered many a subtle method of salesmanship, but none so cunning, so inescapable as this. We have accepted the *Sharif's* hospitality, we have been played to in his court and eaten his food and drunk his tea: now we must pay for it. And, by Allah and all his saints, how we pay! When we attempt to choose the least expensive object which might be useful to us, something at perhaps twenty-five francs, the *Sharif* takes it gently but firmly from us, throws it with a gesture of contempt into a rubbish heap in a corner, as being a paltry object not worthy of the notice of two such eminent visitors, and hands us something which could be no possible use to us but costs two hundred francs.

He is overwhelmingly courteous, but he is

inexorable. He knows that by all the laws of hospitality and of human nature there is no escape for us. Nor do we attempt to escape without buying: our efforts are directed only towards getting away without being reduced entirely to beggary.

It costs us one hundred and thirty francs, the hospitality of this *Sharif*, this descendant of the Prophet Mahomet. And when we have been gracefully ushered out, and stand alone and deserted in the crowded alley, feeling a little feeble and overwhelmed by this devastating salesmanship, we stand a moment looking at each other before uncontrollable laughter carries us away and brings forgiveness to the *Sharif*.

Later we heard more of this distinguished man. He is the envy of many less enterprising traders in Fez. Every guide in the city has an arrangement whereby he receives twenty-five per cent on the purchases of visitors whom he takes to see the treasures of the *Sharif*. This is a high percentage: with most traders the commission seldom rises above ten or fifteen per cent. But by using his hospitable home in this cunning fashion, the *Sharif* can charge exorbitant prices and so pay a higher percentage, which ensures that no innocent abroad shall be allowed to escape his friendship . . .

"You see how useful it is to be related to a prophet," says the Spirit when we have recovered from our laughter and wander on.

We are still lost in the maze of this city of fantasy. But we do not care; we trust to chance that we shall emerge somewhere, sometime. We have not yet learned that the maze of Fez is more difficult to escape from than any labyrinth that Theseus knew. Its chaos of covered streets and alleys and *souks*, never free from their bewildering streams of restless, hushed humanity, creates too great a puzzle for the uninitiated to solve.

We encounter no more friendly *Sharifs*; we are ignored now, and pass among a people who might not be aware of our existence; a serious people, pale-faced since they seldom feel the sun or the strong light of day. There is no laughter here, no joyous savagery as in bloody Meknes. The citizens of sacred Fez are conscious of their superiority to the rest of mankind; dwelling in this ancient centre of Moorish culture, they cannot forget the greatness of their dead past.

Only once do we glimpse the fanaticism that lies beneath the surface of their apparent unconcern. We hear the chant of many childish voices which tells of the nearness of a Koranic school, and the way takes us to its arched entrance. In the dim interior some thirty small boys sit on Moorish rugs on the floor. Their round dark heads are shaven, like the heads of all Moorish boys, and from the crown of each hangs a six-inch pigtail. Its purpose is to enable Allah's blind Angel of Death to pull them up to Paradise if they should die young. Each boy holds a copy of the Holy Book, from which all in unison chant monotonously and endlessly the truths that Allah revealed to Mahomet. In the centre of the group sits the teacher, holding a long switch with which he gives an occasional whack to the head of a child whose attention strays from the Koran.

As we pause at the arched doorway the chanting ceases and a sudden silence falls on the school. Thirty pairs of eyes are turned towards us, not in curiosity, not in friendliness, but in hostility. The teacher sits like a stone image, his switch idle, his eyes set upon us in a bright, expressionless stare. For a full half-minute it seems as though the school has turned itself into a tableau for our entertainment, so immovable are these dim figures.

Then one of the boys nearest the door lowers his

head and spits viciously at our feet. It is the sign of his contempt for the unbeliever. Another boy follows his example, and a third; and there is no reproof from the teacher.

For a moment more we gaze at each other, this school whose religion teaches intolerance and hatred, and we two unbelievers who would like to tell them that we respect any man's religion, so long as it brings him consolation. Then we turn away. Not until we are out of sight do we hear the chant of the Koran again.

The day is waning now, we have had no food except mint tea and almond cakes, and we feel it is time we returned to our temporary home in the Valley of the Nightingales. It is not wise to remain in Fez at night. Sections of the city are enclosed by vast gates, which are shut when darkness falls; we have no wish to be imprisoned in the labyrinth. Yet we do not know which way to turn.

Candles are being lighted now in some of the shops, where the traders sit cross-legged reading their Korans now that the day's business is nearly over. We have to crouch back into doorways to make way for mules and asses, laden with sacks of charcoal, which move swiftly through the dim narrow ways, their passing made the more mysterious by the complete silence of their hooves on the soft earth. As we step into one arched doorway there is a shout from a passing Moor, who waves us away: we have almost polluted the sanctity of a mosque.

"I think," says the Spirit, "we must really make an effort to get out before we do anything that involves us in a pogrom or whatever they have for Christians."

We decide to ask the first likely youth we meet to guide us to the Bab Bou Jeloud, which is the gate nearest to our hotel. Yet it is hard to find idlers in this busy place, where everybody seems to be intent on some secretive affair. Presently we see our youth lounging against a shop.

After a brief spell of bargaining he agrees to take us for three francs. He leads for fifty yards through twists and turns of the streets, and lo, we emerge at the gate. Alone, we might have wandered for hours without finding it.

3

We have an invitation. It is from Hadji Youssef ben Tayyib, an eminent *caid* of Fez, whose honourable prefix of "hadji" shows that he has made the holy pilgrimage to Mecca. His invitation, delivered in answer to our note of introduction sent to him yesterday morning, is written in French in a carefully cultivated handwriting but with the flowery diction of Arabic. Later we discovered the reason. Youssef is an elderly man who speaks French but has never learned to write it, so he dictated the invitation in Arabic to his more scholarly son, who translated it into French, retaining the father's diction. He says : —

"*To the noble and distinguished Monsieur Gordon West* et femme — *The days of our lives are made happier by your presence, and there is joy in the house of Youssef ben Tayyib that the friends of his friend will soon be sheltered by his roof, which praise be to Allah is hospitable to all who come from far places. To-morrow after the setting of the sun Youssef ben Tayyib will prepare for you a feast, and his house shall be your house, and his servants your servants, for so long as you may desire. The son of Youssef ben Tayyib will wait upon you at your hotel and bring you to his house.*"

We are charmed by this flowery invitation. It has all the romantic colourful exaggeration that we would expect from this centre of Arab culture and magnificence. When we have translated it into English, the

Spirit sits on her balcony and rolls it off her tongue again and again, revelling in its cadences . . .

We are ready and waiting, then, for the son of Youssef ben Tayyib. We have no indication of the hour of his calling. We seek enlightenment from *madame* of the hotel, but she cannot help. She shrugs and says that these people have no sense of time; it might be six o'clock or it might be eight. They do not dine, these Moors, until half-past nine or ten o'clock, which to her is an hour very fantastic.

It is almost eight o'clock when a two-horsed barouche arrives at the garden gate and a young Moor steps out. He wears a pale mauve *djellab* and a fez. He is a handsome youth, with a pale olive complexion and bright liquid brown eyes that glow with a kind of shy friendliness as he touches our hands and raises his own to his lips. In excellent French he asks after our health and wishes us prosperity. He explains that he has come from the house of his father to escort us.

Soon we are clattering away in the barouche. The Spirit and I sit side by side on the rear seat, with the son of our host opposite. He does not talk a great deal, but contents himself with occasionally pointing out something which he thinks may interest us. For the most part he looks at us with the unembarrassed interest of a child, sometimes giving us a quiet smile of friendliness. He tells us his name is Hassan, which means "the Good" or the "Beautiful." He asks us our opinion of Fez, and we tell him it is the most wonderful, the most romantic city we have seen. He is gratified and a little surprised, for he has heard that London and Paris are so much more wonderful, with trains that run under the streets and many other strange things.

It is no easy matter to give an impression of London to this young man, who has never been out

of Morocco nor seen any modern towns more
elaborate than those which the French have built in
his country.

We drive for two miles or more along the winding,
hilly road which for twelve miles circles the walls of
Fez. The sun has set, the song of the nightingale
begins to rise from the valleys, storks on roof-tops are
clattering their beaks with a sound like the mirthless
laughter of witches. This city was not built for
carriages, so that no vehicle can enter it, but must go
by roundabout ways to the gate nearest the house of
destination.

Presently we turn into one of the great gateways
and Hassan pays off the carriage. He leads us through
tortuous ways, dimly lighted now with hanging
electric lamps installed by the French, until we arrive
at a mean doorway where a hooded beggar crouches,
pleading for alms in a high wailing chant. I drop a
few centimes into a skinny outstretched hand, remem-
bering that charity is one of the tenets of the Moslem
faith.

Beyond the mean door we enter a courtyard whose
loveliness in the twilight surpasses that of any we have
yet seen. It is tiled in blue and white, and panelled
with a fretwork of exquisite Moorish carvings. Amid
a cluster of orange trees a fountain rises from a great
blue and green basin. The splashing of its water is
the only sound in this secluded world.

Beyond the fountain is a pillared, arched doorway covered by a blue curtain, beside which a negro
" slave " stands like an ebony statue. He draws aside
the curtain, giving a big genial white smile as we pass,
and we enter a chamber of even greater loveliness. It
has a floor of golden-brown cedarwood; pillars of
the same material support a ceiling trellised with a
pattern of crimson and blue. Beside the white marble
walls are low divans covered with Moorish rugs in

patterns of red and blue, and the centre of the floor is spread with coloured rugs on which are scattered a profusion of silken cushions.

Youssef ben Tayyib advances to greet us, kissing his hand after the touch of friendship. He is a tall man of great dignity, with a pale parchment skin and the white beard of a patriarch. He wears a pale blue gown whose colour shows faintly through an overslip of fine transparent muslin, and his head is adorned with a very large white turban.

He has an exquisite courtesy and the manner of a caliph of eastern romance. He wishes us prosperity and peace of mind, and gravely asks how we have fared in our travels and whither we are bound. We assure him of our happiness in Morocco, and after a further exchange of small-talk he excuses himself with a gesture and walks over to a great brass kettle which steams on a glowing charcoal brazier set in a bronze tray. Beside it is a low cedarwood table which carries glasses and sprigs of fresh mint. He busies himself for a while, brewing the ceremonial tea, pouring it boiling on to the mint, until its fragrance pervades the room. Moorish hospitality decrees that the host must always wait upon his guests.

We are joined now by another patriarch who proves to be the brother of Youssef, and again we go through the customary greetings, Hassan invites us to sit, and himself slips gracefully down on to the cushions, after stepping out of his shoes and leaving them at the edge of the rug.

Now a Moor always uncovers his feet when he sits down to refreshment; and although he will make allowances for the barbarous customs of foreigners, he nevertheless appreciates their observance of his own etiquette. So we, too, remove our shoes before we dispose ourselves on the cushions.

For me it is a simple matter to sit cross-legged in

the Moorish fashion, but for the Spirit there is the problem of skirts. She decides that the best position for herself is a kind of side-saddle lounge. We manage fairly successfully, yet I must confess that we cannot achieve the same grace as do those whose customs we are imitating. Our clothes, which in these exotic surroundings seem barbarous in comparison with the soft flowing garments of our hosts, do not lend themselves to such negligent postures.

But there can be no embarrassment in the friendly atmosphere created by these two old men and the youth Hassan. Youssef himself hands round the glasses of fragrant tea, of which it is customary to drink three glasses before a meal; and we sit talking, or sometimes we are silent and meditative.

In Moorish hospitality the hiatus in conversation brings no embarrassment; there is no need to maintain the perpetual exchange of words without which an Occidental dinner party would be considered a failure. If we have something to say, we speak; if we prefer silent communion, we can remain mute and say afterwards, as Carlisle once said to Emerson, that we have had a grand night.

Youssef's brother is interested in political matters, and asks about the politics of England. I try to explain to him the workings of our party methods, but find it hard to make him understand. When I have ended a discourse which I believe to have been a simple and lucid exposition of the system, he reveals a complete lack of comprehension by asking why the party which is in power does not imprison all the other parties who oppose them. His mentality is still of the Middle Ages, and he cannot understand why supreme power should tolerate opposition.

Hassan knows better: he explains to his uncle that in Western countries, where the people vote for their governments, they do not imprison men for their politics, but only for crimes against the State, for theft, and killings, and for marrying more than one wife at the same time. Therein he reveals the divergence that is growing between the old generation and the new in Morocco: the one still bound by a mediaeval past, the other absorbing western ideas through the alien occupation of the French . . .

And now there is a diversion. Three Moorish musicians enter the outer court and sit in a row facing the wide arched doorway. One has a three-stringed *guenbri*, the second a fiddle, which he sets upright on one knee to play, the third carries a tambourine. They strike up a queer little high-pitched, barbaric tune, and they are very mournful about it. Presently the man with the tambourine breaks into a shrill wailing song, to which the music throbs and quavers and squeals, sometimes coming to a sudden pause, then leaping on again. We do not understand his words, but Hassan translated them for me afterwards, and I wrote them down. He told me the song was a popular Berber love chant many centuries old.

> *My love was like a young gazelle,*
> *Her eyes when she looked upon me*
> *Made me to hide my own in the dark*
> *For they were brighter than the sun shining in water,*
> *My love had breasts*
> *Rounder than the pomegranates*
> *That made me desire to pluck them,*
> *My love had lips*
> *Redder than a flower*
> *And her skin was whiter than milk,*
> *My love had feet*
> *Smaller than petals of the jasmine*
> *And swifter than the feet of an antelope,*
> *So that she fled away and escaped me;*
> *But when her eyes were turned the other way from me*
> *I was no longer dazzled but could see,*

*And my legs became longer than the legs of a
    camel . . .
My love is like a flower that I have gathered,
And she is mine.*

When the song is ended and we have all expressed
our delight to the host and his musicians, Youssef rises
and disappears through a massive arched door at the
end of the hall. He has gone to superintend
the preparation of the dinner. Presently he returns,
followed by two negro servants. One places in the
centre of our circle a carved table of cedarwood,
standing on thick legs six inches high; the other
deposits on it a big wooden platter covered by a high
cone-shaped basket.

The first negro circles with a bowl of warm
rosewater, in which we dip our hands and dry them
on perfumed towels. Youssef passes round a basket
of bread, the cover is lifted from the platter, and two
exquisitely-browned roast fowl are revealed. Youssef
takes bread, dips it in the gravy and sonorously intones
the Moslem grace "*Bismillah*," which means that we
are about to eat by the grace of Allah. We follow his
example. Then Youssef, holding a crusty piece of
bread between thumb and second finger, using his
first finger as a clamp, deftly removes a morsel of
the bird and offers it to my mouth, which accepts it.
No knives or forks or spoons are used at a Moorish
table; and it is the custom for the host to feed the
most savoury pieces of a dish to his guest, and for
friend to offer them to friend. Youssef presents
another choice piece to the Spirit, who receives it with
upturned face and open mouth, like a young bird
being fed at the nest.

When we as guests have tasted, all five of us
concentrate on the fowls, pulling them to pieces,
eating rapidly in silence, and occasionally offering each
other the very special scraps. The bones we toss back

into the platter, our hands we wipe on small napkins.

The half-finished dish is removed and another takes its place. This time we have a brace of wild duck, stuffed with richly flavoured rice and herbs and served with a salad of orange, radish and raisins.

Youssef tears the birds asunder and we help ourselves and each other. Hassan seems to have made the Spirit his special charge, perhaps because he is more modern than his elders, to whom women are of so little account that they are not allowed to dine with the men of the household: it is only because the Spirit is a guest and a foreigner that she is permitted to be present. Under the attentions of Hassan, who is continually offering her the best morsels he can find, her mouth is never empty. Hassan leans back with a little smile of pleasure each time she accepts, and I know she has not the heart to refuse him, even though by this time she had eaten enough.

The remains of the ducks are wafted away and placed before the now silent musicians, who fall to with enthusiasm. Drinking water is passed round in small bronze bowls while another dish is laid before us. We are faced now with a great roast of mutton. Like the fowls and the ducks, it is so tender through long, slow cooking that we have no difficulty in pulling it to pieces with our fingers.

The next course brings us more variety. It is *couscous*, the national dish of Morocco. It is said to be an importation from Provence, brought over by the Barbary pirates in the twelfth century. The communal bowl contains a great mound of steamed semolina, in the centre of which is a crater filled with a rich stew. There are scraps of chicken and tender lamb, young capsicums and small green tomatoes, barley-sprouts and almonds, and laid on top of this for a covering are green haricot beans capped by a sprinkling of raisins.

Although this may sound to be a terrifying dish, I can assure you that it is delicious. Our chief difficulty is in eating it. This requires a great deal of practice. You dip into the dish, make your selection, roll it deftly with the fingers in the palm of the hand, binding it into a rough ball with the semolina, and slip it into the mouth. Hassan gives us a demonstration, and we admire the ease with which he manipulates his material. Our own attempts are watched with extreme gravity by the elders, and with laughing delight by Hassan, who at length succeeds in coaching us into making at least a presentable show of this difficult art.

By this time we are almost overcome by the quantities of food we have eaten, yet there is more to come. There is a dish of rich sweet pastries, and of crisp almond cakes and dates, followed by a platter of grapes. We begin to dread the removal of each dish, knowing that it will make room for another. But an end is reached at last, our hands are washed in the circulating bowl, and we lean back in our cushions, exhausted. Youssef's brother gives a little belch of wind, which is no vulgarity, but a recognised courtesy designed to show that he has enjoyed his relative's food.

Then Hassan hands round long pipes of *kiff*, the Moorish powdery tobacco which has a perfume of herbs. The pipe has a wooden stem eighteen inches long, finely carved and decorated with colour, with a red clay bowl the size of a small thimble. Youssef passes round more glasses of mint tea while we lounge, smoking and talking between weird arabesques of music, which begin nowhere and end unexpectedly on some high shrill note. Hassan, sitting cross-legged and dreamily playing with his bare toes, begins to chant softly in strange cadences. In the intervals I tell a few of the best stories I can remember after so overpowering a meal, and the Spirit tells some of hers. Hassan can appreciate the point of them all, he throws his head back in laughter and hugs his knees; but the elders lack his sense of humour and his understanding of western ways, thereby again revealing the gulf that is growing between pre- and post-French generations.

So the evening passes until it is after midnight, and we must leave. With many expressions of delight at his entertainment, we take our farewell of Youssef and his brother, receiving in return their wishes for our prosperity and happiness, and Youssef's assurance that his roof is our roof whenever we will grace it with our presence.

With Hassan as our guide we go out into the silent alleys of Fez, past the hooded beggar whose wailing plea is stilled in sleep; past mysterious figures that move swiftly and silently, casting fantastic shadows in the vague light of the electric lamps; or that lie in the misery and poverty of their rags at the sides of the streets; and so by tortuous ways out of the city to a carriage whose Arab driver lies asleep in the seat we are to occupy. Hassan insists that he shall come with us to the hotel door; and before we part we have accepted his invitation to go adventuring with him on other days into the secret places of Fez . . .

The song of a thousand nightingales rises to our windows as we sink drowsily to our beds in the early hours, at peace with life and the world, tranquil with the sense of friendship which we have brought away from these charming people.

We are well satisfied with our first experience of Moorish hospitality; and of one thing we are very sure — that so long as we live we shall never again need to eat.

4

Many days and nights we spent with Hassan and his friends, exploring the mysteries of Fez; enchanted by the glories of its architecture, distressed by the degradation and poverty of its people; fascinated by the rich cultural life of its *medersas*; intrigued by its vices; filled with wonder by its crude superstitions and childish sorceries. In Fez we are at the fountain-head of a civilisation that has passed its zenith and is now moving inexorably in its decline. The ancient glories conceived by its great rulers in the days of their riches and power survive to-day as a lovely and fantastic background for its decadence.

Shall I tell of its sorceries?

Hassan, like all strict Moslems, professes not to believe and laughs at them; yet somewhere in his mind I think there is fear. Superstitions that have been handed on for thousands of years cannot die in a generation. He was uneasy, I know, when we visited one of the many *khatats*, who divine the future with sand and shells and the warm blood of cocks, as our own fortune-tellers pretend to divine it by use of cards and crystals.

We saw this *khatat*, a wild, long-haired fanatic with the bright eyes of a madman, receive a man who, desiring to know some secret, crouched trembling on the ground while the seer drew strange cabalistic devices in a pile of minute seashells. He cut the throat of a live fowl and anointed his client with the spurting hot blood; then burned blood in a brazier and with many incantations drew his message out of the blood-created smoke.

We saw other sorcerers who drove out devils with burning irons, and cured simple people of their evil spirits by cupping them and drawing their blood.

We saw women weeping and wailing at the little

white houses that are the tombs of departed saints, kissing the bare walls in an ecstacy of supplication because they desired children but were barren. We saw the blood of a sacrificed goat ceremonially mixed with the foundations of a house that was being built, so that evil spirits should not be able to enter; and the black hand of Fatima, daughter of Mahomet, painted on the wall to charm away evil.

Shall I tell of vices?

One night I went with Hassan to the House of the Dancing Boys, where rich Moors jaded by many wives and concubines reclined at their ease, smoking hashish in their *kiff* pipes, while youths of the Chleuh or Berber tribes of the south danced sensuously for their delight to the shrill wail of the African flute and the throb of the drum.

The melting, inviting eyes of these small Sons of Delight are darkened with kohl, their faces are delicately made up, and they wear the garments of girls. They dance with a lithe grace, with many beckoning smiles and suggestive movements that hold the intent, hungry gaze of their fascinated audience.

Between the dances these little perverts minister to the needs of their admirers, serving them with tea, filling their pipes, and receiving in return caresses such as a woman might receive from a man she has fascinated. And sometimes one of the guests will depart through the curtained doorway to another part of the house with the dancer of his choice.

Yet there is no self-consciousness about these proceedings; one has a feeling of their inevitability, as though they are a natural part of the life of the people . . .

Shall I tell of dreamy, tranquil hours?

Of days idled away in the magnificence of the Palais Jamai and its terraced gardens, where fountains play amid the orange trees, and great white tree-lilies delight the eye, and the perfume of jasmine enchants the senses?

It stands, this Palace, on the edge of the labyrinth, and we reach it after a three-mile drive around the ancient walls. A few years ago it was the home of one of the great families of Fez on whom disaster fell, swift and brutal, like all African tragedy. To-day it is an hotel, where we may wander from the Hall of Audience, ornate with all the lavish skill and artifice of Moorish architecture, to the once-forbidden harem, where we lounge on divans and take coffee and gaze through a great grille of wrought iron to the city which lies like a jumble of white boxes in the valley below, rising on either side of the hills that encompass it.

While we lounge here, Hassan tells us the story of the Jamai brothers who built this palace to house their magnificence and power. Maati ed Jamai was once Grand Vizier of the Empire, and his brother was Minister of War. They had an enemy and rival in the ruthless Ba Ahmed, son of a slave, half-negro and half-Jew, yet Chamberlain of the Sultan Mulai Hassan. So long as Sultan Hassan lived, the Jamai brothers were all powerful, but when he died, and his weak son Abd-el-Aziz succeeded, Ba Ahmed had his chance.

Ba Ahmed poisoned the mind of Abd-el-Aziz, and when one day Maati ed Jamai was summoned to the Presence, Ba Ahmed accused him to the Sultan of all manner of disloyalties, asking permission to arrest him. So Maati ed Jamai, who had entered the royal presence as the most powerful man in Morocco, was dragged out in chains amid the jeers of the populace.

For ten years he lived in the dungeons of Tetuan, chained to his brother; and his palace in which we now sit was confiscated. At last Maati died, and for two weeks his brother remained chained to the corpse. Four years later, in 1908, he was released, a broken, penniless man, his great possessions gone, his family dead from want and persecution. And to-day Abd-el-Aziz, the Sultan whose word sealed his fate, lives on the Mountain in Tangier — an exile . . .

Then there are days when we laze in the warm shade of gardens, beside streams and pools where water tortoises paddle their ungainly bodies among floating lilies, while we play cards with Hassan and his friends. They favour a kind of poker, with cards that carry queer Moorish inscriptions and fantastic pictures in place of clubs and spades and hearts.

One languid afternoon we liven up the placid hour by teaching our friends to play " snap "; and so great an excitement does this nursery game arouse that our group is soon surrounded by a crowd who must learn the reason for all this shouting.

When we pass the garden next day, we find that the players have adopted the new game. Excited cries of " znap " echo from the shady places, and there is no longer peace in the garden.

Very friendly and happy days they are, so that when the time comes for us to move on we are reluctant to drag ourselves away. But a morning comes when, soon after dawn, we are again packing ourselves into a bus, with Hassan smiling a farewell, and the Spirit nursing a *pastilla*, a great round pastry packed with meat and chicken and eggs and powdered with cinnamon, which is a parting gift from the kitchen of Youssef ben Tayyib and his son.

CHAPTER 6.

Tells of an Imperial Highway — Village of the Acacias —
Berber Homes — Walk in the Mountains — New Friends
— the Epic of Moha Hammou — Journey through the Forest
— the Room of the Gay Lady — Thé Dansant in the
Wilderness — Café Occidental — a Night Out with Harry
the Legionnaire — Foreign Legion — Gay Lady Returns.

I

The road on which we speed through Meknes
towards Azrou, our next stopping place Sahara-wards,
is the old Imperial Highway of Morocco. Along it in
the past have come Sultans with their retinues and
their armies, bringing back slaves and gold and great
riches from the South; caravans which have travelled
many moons from the Sudan and far Timbuktu with
treasures for the Moorish overlords. To-day shining
cars speed over its well-kept surface, Moors on
bicycles pedal their way in and out of the towns, and
the only caravans we meet consist of half a dozen
donkeys burdened with mountains of firewood and
charcoal, or lorries carrying factory-made merchandise
and iron ore. Instead of the wild armies of Sultans
we meet a column of men of the Foreign Legion on
the march from the mountains, and a few rusty tanks
being transported on lorries.

We are climbing now into the lower slopes of the
Middle Atlas mountains, and beyond them we shall
mount again and scale the more formidable heights of
the Grand Atlas. We pass first through a country
which men have called the Landscape of the Moon, a
chaos of tortured mountain ridges and peaks, volcanic
and barren, and soon we are among the green hills on
which white flocks of sheep graze, and the long, low

black tents of the great Berber tribe of the Beni
M'guild, who have camped here for seven hundred
years, spread themselves across the verdure like giant
bats come to earth with outstretched wings. We make
a few stops at villages where our driver delivers a
handful of mail; but for the most part the journey is
uneventful, and half our travelling companions, those
same aloof French colonials with a sprinkling of
Moors, are nodding into sleep, wearied by the constant
changing of gears, the drone of engines and the
warmth of the bus.

When we have travelled some eighty miles we
begin to climb steeply, and soon the bus swings round
a final twist in the mountain road into Azrou. We
alight at a dingy café-hotel which also is the booking
office for the bus, and are at once surrounded by a
rabble of small boys offering porterage. There is
dazzling sunshine here, at an altitude of more than
three thousand feet, but a fresh invigorating wind
carries the chill of snow from the higher slopes, so
that I am glad of the overcoat which I reluctantly
brought under pressure from the Spirit, who is wiser
than I in these matters.

The Spirit does not like the look of this café-
hotel, so we give our scanty luggage to a ragged
Berber youth and ask him to take us to the next, if
there is one. We follow him up the village street
into a triangular open space which at home would
be the village green. White dolls' houses with roofs
of shining green tiles enclose it, trees heavy with
white acacia droop to meet masses of snowy irises
that grow from the ochre-tinted earth. This is
the new French village which has risen among the
mountains. Away to the right the Berber village of
yellow boxes climbs tier by tier up the green mountain-
side.

Far and away, in a great semi-circle beyond, rise

vast woods of evergreen oaks, and beyond those the forests of cedars.

Our hotel proves to be an inn built of red concrete, with a loggia opening on the village green. It is kept by a French family, a tired mother with two lively daughters and a son. It has a bare stone interior, with a dining room on one side, a darts parlour and bar on the other, and in the centre a wide stone staircase which leads up to eight or nine bedrooms. We become the tenants of two stone chambers which give on to an upper loggia amid the fragrance of the acacia trees. The air here has a cold purity that exhilarates and sharpens the appetite, so that in spite of our incursions into Hassan's vast *pastilla*, we are eager for dinner when we go downstairs.

A fire of logs blazes in the open hearth of the dining room, even though we are well into the month of May; for summer comes late and departs early in these altitudes. We gather round the lambent flames with the two daughters and the son of the house, and wait hungrily while the mother busies herself preparing the meal. She is sunken-eyed and has the marks of hard labour on her weary face, which softens and brightens when she joins her children for a few minutes during her cooking. She caresses her son affectionately before hurrying back to her labours, while the daughters delve into the latest dress catalogues from Meknes and Rabat, discussing this and that creation. They are pretty girls of nineteen or so, and they are content to let their weary mother slave away her life while they dream of the clothes they would like to wear. They tell us they have lived here all their lives and have never been to their own country. They would like to go to Paris, they would like to go anywhere from Azrou; they are bored with the place, for there is nothing to do and nowhere to go, except to Meknes by the bus. Meknes is their metropolis, with its cinema and its shops and restaurants. There are young men at Meknes, too.

We dine well on a good vegetable soup, trout from the mountain lakes, artichokes, grilled cutlets, a fine dish of beans, oranges, apples, nuts and a flask of good strong red Meknassi. There are two other guests, a middle-aged man who sits with the family, speaks scarcely a word, and goes out when he has finished eating, and a non-commissioned officer from the French outpost in the village. He tells us he has been here a year and is sick of the place; he wants to get back to Rabat, where he had been stationed before. There, well — one finds a little life; here, what is there for a man to do except eat and sleep?

When dinner is over we join the family party. The daughters are still busy with their catalogues, whose coloured illustrations fascinate them. The son is busy preparing his skis to be put away for the summer. He is sorry the snows are over, for there is good sport higher up the mountains. Only a few miles away is Ifrane, which the French have developed into a winter sports resort for the people of the cities. It's a place to live in, Ifrane, he says, with its fine hotels. One of them has as many as a hundred bedrooms.

Presently we go out into the village, dimly lighted now by a few street lamps which are hopelessly outshone by a moon whose exuberance suggests that it is bursting with its own light. An icy wind sweeps down from the cedar forests, driving us indoors. When we go to bed we have to pile our clothes on top of the bed-clothes to keep ourselves warm.

Morocco, in the mountains, in May.

2

When the sun is up in the morning there is warmth in Azrou. And there is a friendliness among its people which we have not encountered before in Morocco.

The Berber tribesmen and women whom we meet when we wander out through the village give us grave smiles and greetings; and there is a blessed absence of touts and guides and hangers-on.

Once only did an Azrouan seek money from us, and he gave value for it beforehand. We were stepping through the muddy streets when he appeared suddenly in front of us, bowed, then began to turn rapid double and treble somersaults, cartwheels, hand-springs, and all manner of acrobatic contortions. He was a small boy of perhaps twelve years, dressed in the traditional red and yellow clothes of the Moroccan acrobat. It was an astonishing exhibition to be suddenly offered in the middle of a street in a mountain village. When he had finished, the boy gave us a happy grin and held out his small skull-cap for the reward; and when he received a franc, which was high pay, he did not even demand more, which was almost a phenomenon. We asked him about himself, and he told us that he was going to be one of the most famous acrobats in the world. He would travel the world in a circus and would make much money, by the grace of Sidi Ahmed.

Now Sidi Ahmed ou Moussa is the patron saint of acrobats, whose disciples are to be found not only in Morocco, but in foreign circuses all over the world. You will see them performing in many of the market places and squares of Morocco. Mostly they come from the Souss, away in the hot south down by Agadir.

We wished our youthful aspirant good luck, and told him we would come to see him when he performed in London. He said he would look out for us!

Higher up we pass the cobbler, who is a versatile man. He sits at the side of the street, with his paraphernalia around him, prepared to mend your shoes while you wait; and he will also shoe your mule or your horse, it is all the same to him. His instruments are a knife, a hammer and a needle and thread; his stock a few scraps of leather and felt and a score of iron horse-shoes of varying sizes.

Further on we pause to study the primitive huts of the Berbers. They are built of mountain stone and mud, with small square windows outlined in blue paint and covered by rough wrought-iron grilles. The doors are hand-made and seldom close properly; roofs consist of a foot of earth, on which some of the occupants grow corn and vegetables.

As we pause to look inside one of these primitive homes, the housewife comes to the door, smiles in greeting, and seeing our interest invites us in. Her home has two rooms. The family bed is a bank of hard earth with a few coarse bright-coloured Berber rugs thrown upon it. Her table consists of a solid circular piece of wood sliced from one of the great cedars of the mountains, standing on three legs about six inches high. She has a rack, brightly decorated in petunia and silver, in which she keeps the communal wooden food bowls, and there is a decorated chest, and a clay fire-oven in which she cooks. Here is extreme poverty allied with cheerfulness and friendliness. We admire her goods and chattels, and she enjoys our appreciation, though she does not understand a word we say, for she speaks only the Berber dialect. But with smiles and gestures and sounds, the Spirit conveys her admiration for the primitive decorations; and the Berber woman returns the smiles and is clearly happy that we find something of interest in her poor home.

When we pass out into the village street, women who have returned from the pasture lands and the fields are making their toilet. Their dressing table is the earth, their washing bowl usually a tin can or an earthen bowl. One of them is filling a petrol tin at a stream which runs down the street, and dipping her hands and feet in the water.

Down at the bottom of the town we find another kind of village, a large square compound of hard yellow mud. On two sides live many families in conditions of distressing squalor; on the other two sides are the cattle and horses, in hovels in which conditions are little worse than those in which their owners live.

But further on in the valley there is the loveliness of a swift, sparkling mountain river, its banks over-hung by white roses and shaded by limes whose leaves shine silver-grey in the sun. We sit to rest on an old stone bridge. Below, a group of Berber shepherds are washing vast quantities of newly-shorn sheep's wool in the running water, and a crowd of Berber girls lean over the parapet exchanging laughter and jokes with the toilers. Away to the right the red-brown rocks are covered with half an acre of this wool, spread out to dry in the sun. On the left of the stream's bank is a cluster of the white villas of French settlers, and a small Catholic church surmounted by a vast stone cross on which two storks, oblivious of the fact that they are sacred birds of Islam, have committed the heresy of building their crude nest of sticks. The church walls and steps are white with the evidence of their presence, and the Spirit suggests that perhaps, after all, there is method in their heresy: they have settled here so that they can show their contempt for Christianity. Wild pigeons and doves flutter among the limes, cuckoos call in the distance, a hawk or two hover far away over the mountains. Spring has come to this African valley . . .

We lunch on a *kabob* and a glass of mint tea in the village and start out to climb the mountain road towards the forests. It winds up through great rolling slopes where the black tents are pitched. Far below and all around we see white, slow-moving patches which are flocks of sheep, creeping across the verdure of the hills; and here and there moves a black patch which is a herd of goats. Away and away to the plains and the cities this vast panorama of hills and valleys carries the eye; and there is a great solitude, and a silence broken only by the dim *tinka-tinka* of a far-off sheep bell, or by the shrill wail of some Berber song from the ilex woods.

We lie here in the sun, meditating on this strange white race whose origin has always been so shrouded in uncertainty. Some claim the Berbers are the descendants of one of the sons of Noah; but of one thing ethnologists seem to have little doubt — that they are Celts, cousins of those whom we now call Scots and Irish and Basques.

Down in the cities of the plains they have intermarried with Arab and Jew, and before that with Phoenician and Goth, so that their main characteristics have been lost; but up here in the mountains they have kept the purity of their stock, and we look into many a pair of blue or hazel eyes and see many a head of fair or brown hair.

There is the sound of the Celt in their names, too, for we find many a "mac" among them. This tribe we are among now is the M'Guild, and there is also the M'Gills and the M'Tears. I have also heard of a MacKenza; and further along these mountains, among the Zaian people, there is a considerable family named O'Hummo; while in the south one of the three great Lords of the Atlas is a M'Tougi.

These Celtic Berbers, who once possessed the whole of North Africa, were here long before the Romans or the Arabs; and until the coming of the French none could dislodge them from their mountain fastness. Moulay Ismail the Bloody tried and failed, though he managed to impress himself upon Azrou by building a *kasbah* or fortress whose walls still remain. The Romans gave them up as a bad job. As fighters they have been superb; as raiders and bandits, when they have swept down to the plains, ravaging and killing, they have been merciless. For centuries fighting has been their favourite pastime, either united against a common enemy or in tribal warfare among themselves. Multitudes of them fought under the banners of Rome; they predominated in the hordes that conquered Spain; and this same tribe of M'Guild, which spreads its ten thousand black tents from Azrou far across the Middle Atlas, created the great Almohade dynasty of Sultans who ruled in the twelfth and thirteenth centuries.

Little more than twenty years ago they rose under a great chief, Moha Hammou, against the encroachments of the French, and for the first time in their history lost their most coveted possession — complete independence. To-day there are no more bloody raids down to the plains; the elders who rule the tribes have learned the wisdom of obeying the Frenchman's laws against pillage and murder.

We find it hard to credit these proudly-walking courteous people, who tend their flocks and live mainly on goats' milk and grain, with the atrocities they are known to have committed in the past; even though we know that there are few lengths to which men will go in defence of their liberties . . .

The departing sun was setting the mountain ridges and the clouds aflame when we reached the village again. We walked through the gardens where the iris blooms, and beneath the acacias we encountered two men sitting together on a stone seat hand-in-hand, a sign of their friendship.

In these lands of the Arab and the Berber you will often see men holding each other's hands as they walk or sit together; they find their happiest recreation in the contemplation of lovely gardens and in talk beside quiet waters. We were surprised when these two men rose to salute us and bid us good evening; we returned the salute and paused to talk.

They were fine-looking men of perhaps forty, robed in the unsullied white *burnouses* of the prosperous; their brown faces beardless, their eyes large and limpid brown, and calm with a great peace of mind.

One of them, speaking in French, asked if we were staying long in Azrou, and I answered that we would like to stay many days, since not for a long time had we seen so much beauty or known such peace. He was pleased with our praise and told us we would always be welcome in Azrou. We asked if he lived here, and he told us that he was the owner of many sheep. We told him of what we had seen and admired in Azrou, and presently he asked if we would visit his house. We were happy.

The friend took his leave, kissing his hand as they parted, and we walked down the street with our new acquaintance to a house in the village. It is a small house in the Moorish style, with a white inner court, where we sit on mats while our host prepares the customary mint tea. A shy Berber boy who is his son hovers around and presently sits near us, watching us with a natural undisguised curiosity, for we are new kinds of creatures to him. The French he knows, but the English are a dim and faraway people with whom he has not come into contact.

So we pass away a peaceful hour while our host talks softly in answer to our questions. I am curious to know whether the tribes have become resigned to the French occupation of their mountain. He says that the younger generation are content, but many of the older men, those who knew the freedom of the past, are full of dissatisfaction, now that they are no longer permitted to raid their neighbours. For raids meant greater prosperity, and fighting was part of their lives. Himself, he was fighting against the French as a youth; but to-day he would not have conditions otherwise. He gives us to understand that French domination has brought greater and safer prosperity to the prosperous, but has done little good to the poor.

The talk goes back to the wars of the past, and he tells us of the end of Moha Hammou, the last chief to resist in these regions. It is a modern epic in the history of the Middle Atlas. This fierce old leader fought till the last. He was driven from his stronghold at Kenifra, some fifty miles away, but held the tribes together against the common enemy until it became apparent to all but himself that the end was near.

A day came when the sons of Moha decided to make their peace with the invaders, and went to their father to urge him to do the same. But the old man refused.

Make peace with the Unbelievers if you must, he told them; I am too old to change my ways.

The sons took their farewell and went over to the French. A few weeks later, with the section of his tribe that remained faithful, Moha Hammou went to battle against the enemy and their new allies, and died fighting against his sons. So ended the last great resistance of the Middle Atlas tribes, giving the French a free hand to pass on to the Grand Atlas for the final victory which did not come till 1933 . . .

When we leave our host, with many mutual expressions of goodwill, there is twilight in the village, and the icy wind is blowing down from the far-off snows, so that we are glad to gather round the wood fire at the inn.

3

There is a great to-do over the booking of our
seats in the bus for the next morning. A large, blonde
Frenchwoman with billows of flesh and golden curls,
who reminds us of an old-time chorus girl gone to
seed, tells us at the café booking-office that it is
impossible to book from here. Oh, monsieur is very
much mistaken if he thinks seats can be booked from
here. Does not the bus come from Meknes to Azrou
before passing on to Midelt, which is our next stop?
Then it is necessary to book one's seats at Meknes,
because the bus might be full at Meknes and stay full
all the way to Midelt and beyond. She had assuredly
known such things to happen; and if there was no
seat, why then, Monsieur and Madame would have to
wait until the next day, when there might be.

Feeling rather helpless, and decidedly crushed by
this discovery of my ignorance which she has forced
upon me, I ask if it is suggested that we should return
to Meknes to book.

But of course not, she says, there is the telephone.
It would cost me four francs.

Now it is an odd thing that I had never thought
of the telephone. When one has lived for some time
among things primitive, away from the usual amenities
of life, one is inclined to forget that there is nearly
always the telephone. I paid over my four francs, and
the large blonde lady had within a few minutes spoken
to Meknes and ascertained that two seats would be
kept for us when the bus arrived at Azrou.

We leave at eight o'clock in the morning. Our
travelling companions this time are a pair of French
Army officers, one of whom has a wife who treats the
world with a cold indifference; a Catholic priest who
pays attention to nothing except the breviary which
he reads unceasingly; a bearded Jew in the black

gabardine and skull cap which is the uniform imposed on his race by the Sultans of the past; a couple of prosperous Berbers, a trooper and two elderly French-women. There is no conversation during the four-hour journey of eighty miles; it seems as though each passenger is unaware of the existence of others.

With much grinding and screaming of gear-changing the bus begins the climb over the mountains. At first we mount through green valleys and plateaux where the black tents are spread, and the flocks and herds wander high up the slopes; but soon we are among the great gorges cut through the cedar forests. For an hour we pass through these towering mountain trees which rise sometimes to a height of a hundred and forty feet. Here and there a group of monkeys, the apes of Barbary, swing in their branches; and once when we round a bend in the tortuous road a school of them scatters and flees into the forest.

At seven thousand feet the air is sharp and clear, the sun blinding. Sometimes when we sweep perilously round the narrow mountain road, a gorge gives a view across the vast expanses of the valleys and we see the far-off peaks of great blue Ayachi lifted twelve thousand feet into an azure sky. We pass near the source of Oum er Rbia, the Mother of Grass, which begins here as a trickling stream and enters the Atlantic near Mazagan, many days journey away, as a great river, refreshing the parched lands on its way.

When we have thundered through the cedar forests the hues change from the greens and whites and greys of high places to the tawny colours of Africa. We begin to descend over rocky roads that jar and jolt the bus. Soon we are in a wilderness of rock, in lion-coloured valleys hemmed in by fantastic red and lavender hills. Far off beyond the coloured hills the snow-peaks send down winds that temper the heat of these valleys of lovely desolation, turning what would be an inferno into a perfect summer day. There is no sight or sound of life in these fastnesses; we have come into a dead and burnt-up world deserted by man.

We reach at last a wide yellow plain where Midelt rises on a low hill, a small town of a blinding whiteness that drives us in search of sun-glasses as soon as we have alighted in the wide dusty square. We find them for four francs apiece in a tumbledown shop near the bus stop. Then we hand our luggage to a cross-eyed negro youth and ask him to take us to an hotel.

It proves to be a bungalow of uninteresting aspect, standing at the corner of cross-roads. On one side is the plain, on the other the inescapable snow-peaks of Ayachi, nearer now, so that when we are out of the sun we need to huddle in our coats to keep from freezing. The hotel is in a state of being reconditioned; the narrow passage which we enter is a chaos of half-peeled-off paper and broken plaster. But the little elderly Frenchwoman who receives us says we are fortunate: there are two rooms undisturbed, the other four are under repair.

One of these vacant rooms is tiled and bare and pleasant; the other all gaudy colour and fripperies. The shabbiness of a once-easy chair is concealed under fat, fluffy swansdown cushions, in the centre of which coloured representations of Mabel-Lucy-Atwell-looking girls make goo-goo eyes at us. On the walls several nude young women, cut from French magazines and framed, offer their charms with expressions that vary from frank invitation to mock retreat. Here and there gaudy dolls sit about, staring lifelessly at us with bland stupidity. Everything that can possibly have a ribbon on it has been given a ribbon; everything that can receive a coloured cover or decoration has received one. There are tawdry gay cushions on the bed; the eiderdown is like a sugar-coated cake. And the wardrobe is locked.

"There can be no doubt about it," says the Spirit, when she has taken a look round, "This is a whore's room."

Now the problem is, who shall have the whore's room? Its effort to be gaudily voluptuous is rather trying to both of us, but I am prepared to sacrifice the more Spartan amenities of the other room if the Spirit would prefer to have it. Yet the Spartan Room looks on to the roadway where trains of laden asses and military cars pass continually with much noise; whereas the Room of the Gay Lady looks on to a court and is silent. Since I can sleep in any kind of a noise and the Spirit must have quiet, she chooses the room of luxury.

But what, says she, about the locked wardrobe? Supposing there is a body in it? Or supposing something that sleeps there by day should come creeping out by night. A *djinn*, for instance?

You will realise that a locked wardrobe in a strange room exercises a peculiar fascination. It stirs one's curiosity. It gives a sinister atmosphere even to the most exaggeratedly feminine room, particularly when the room is in the heart of Morocco.

We assume, of course, that the lady is temporarily absent, perhaps engaged upon some commission that has taken her out of town for a day or two, and that she has left behind her unnecessary clothes. We sit on her bed and speculate as to her appearance. We are both agreed that she is blonde, and we think she is ample, like many of the blonde charmers we have met in Morocco. They seem to grow blonder and ampler, observes the Spirit, as they approach nearer to the Sahara.

While we are thus speculating, the proprietress enters with a jug of hot water for ablutions. The Spirit asks her about the wardrobe, and whether there is a body in it.

Oh, no, she says reassuringly, Oh, no, no, no, madame, but of course not. It is only that the lady who is a regular *locataire* is away for a few days. She regrets, but the lady has the key, so if madame could use the wardrobe in monsieur's room, as it is only for two nights . . .

Our possessions are so few that we do not really need the wardrobe, so we agree to madame's proposal.

Since the hotel does not supply food, we go out in search of it. Madame tells us that across the road is a restaurant, where her guests always go for meals. It is regretted, she says, that the restaurant at the hotel is not yet ready; she hopes that by next year she will have been able to build it.

The place to which she has directed us is pleasant enough, wide and bare and light, with a bar at one end, where two very modern young women minister to the needs and listen to the pleasantries of a group of French officers. In the centre a glass door opens on to a rather dreary-looking ballroom festooned with paper flowers.

Here, says the young Berber waiter who serves us, they have gala nights at the week-ends: all Midelt comes to disport itself. Even now we may dance, he adds, for a *thé dansant* is about to begin. He leads us to yet another room, whence comes the sound of music. A women in a red velvet coat is tump-tumping on a piano, and two forlorn-looking men are sadly squeaking away on violins. One of the barmaids, who is a dance partner in her spare time, is dancing with one of the young officers; otherwise there is plenty of room on the floor. The waiter invites us to dance, since it is long past lunch time and we have to wait for our meal.

"Did we come all this way to dance?" I ask the Spirit.

"We did not," she says. "We came to escape from it."

So we go to the bar for a drink, and are soon in conversation with the young officers. They are puzzled to know why we have come to this God-forsaken place, finding it hard to believe that we were impelled by nothing more than curiosity. There is little of interest in these regions, except mountains and desert and natives, they tell us. Our assurance that to us these things are interesting produce only a shrug. They cannot understand why one should not seek one's interest in Paris or on the Cote d'Azur, or at some place where there are distractions. They have all the longing of exiles for the gay places of the world.

Now, I am interested in the Foreign Legion, some companies of which are stationed at Midelt, and I ask if it is known whether there are any English among the men here. One of the officers believes there may be one or two; though now there are not so many of the English in the Legion. Plenty of Germans and Czechs and Russians, but few English. He gives me to understand that the Legionnaires are beyond the pale of normal humanity. But if I wish to meet any Legionnaires, I will find them at the Café Occidental, their usual haunt in the town.

That evening we found the café. The Spirit remarked that it seemed more accidental than occidental. It was a ramshackle place, resembling one of those saloons of the Wild West beloved of film producers. A few soldiers sat around games of cards with drinks at their sides; a few civilians talked together; a red faced young Air Force corporal in a group played a concertina. The waiter who brought our drinks, answering my enquiry, said he knew of one Englishman who was a fairly frequent customer, though he could not assure us that he would come in to-night. The Legion had received their fortnightly pay a week ago, he explained, and few had any money left by this time. When they have nothing to spend, they do not come to the café. When they have much, they spend it — ah, how they spend it, he said, with a gesture towards our glasses. He promised to tell us if the Englishman arrived.

Ten minutes later he comes over and tells me that the man is here, indicating a Legionnaire who has entered with a group of his fellows.

" Ask him if he will have a drink with us," I tell the waiter.

We watched him deliver the invitation. The man turns towards us, stares as if he could not believe the evidence of his eyes, and comes across to our table almost at a trot.

" Blimy, what a godsend," he says.

" Need a drink as badly as that ?" I ask.

" 's not so much that, guv'nor. I means, seein' someone from 'ome."

" Don't often meet them here ?"

" You bet I don't, not in this perishin' 'ole. Last mate I 'ad that was English tried to make a bolt for it. 'E didn't get far."

I ask him what he will have to drink.

" Earthquake for me," says he.

I order three earthquakes, inquiring what manner of drink this may be. It proves to be a tumbler of strong cheap white wine mixed with *pernod*, producing a concoction which has the kick of a camel. According to our friend it is the favourite drink of the Legion.

The beer's stuff to wash yer socks in, he says. The wine's all right, but not so strong as it might be. Whisky's too dear. A bloke has to have a drink with a kick when he gets down these parts.

He is a little man of perhaps twenty-seven, a rapid-talking vociferous Cockney with a quick grin and a respect for no man. He says his name is Harry

Trussler, but for the truth of this I cannot vouch: it is almost a tradition of the Foreign Legion that men do not enlist under their correct names. He has been two years in this strange, rough regiment composed of half the nationalities of the world — of renegades, of thieves, of honest young men who sought romance and adventure but found only strict discipline and hard work.

"Mind you, it's not such a bad show, if you can 'take it'," he tells us. "But some of 'em can't. Not knowin' the lingo makes it worse, o' course. You 'ave to pick it up as you go along. Me, I c'n talk it pretty good now, but when I come first I didn't know a ruddy word 'cept *van blonk* and *parley voo*. They didn' 'arf take it outer me, too.

"But once you knows yer job and makes up yer mind to stick, it's all right, see? Except being with these foreigners all the time. Not bad blokes, though, some of 'em. But all yer do is work, work, work — makin' roads, diggin', buildin' — anythink except fightin', There ain't no fightin' to do now; they cleaned up 'ere years ago. Now'n again there's a bit of a blow-up between a couple o' tribes in the mountains. Then we goes up to put the kybosh on it. But that don't 'appen often, worse ruddy luck."

A second earthquake was loosening the tongue of Legionary Trussler. We could see that he was enjoying himself, unburdening his soul in his own language, which he had not spoken for many months.

"I've seen blokes come out 'ere full o' fancy ideas, like; thinkin' it was goin' to be all beer and skittles and 'arems. Fat lot of 'arems you can keep, on four francs a day. That's all the pay you gets at first. 'Course, they gives yer more later, if yer don't get into no trouble. But what can yer do, even with four francs a day, I ask yer? When they see what they've let 'emselves in for, some chaps try to make a bolt for it, same as my pal did. An' then they get shoved in chokey, where it's pretty 'ot for 'em."

"Why do most of them join?" the Spirit inquires. I know she wishes to ask him why he is in the Legion, but this is a question one never puts to anybody who belongs to a regiment with a reputation for being the last resource of men who were in disgrace at home.

Trussler takes a pull at his third earthquake and helps himself to the packet of cigarettes on the table.

"They ain't all crooks, if that's what you're thinkin'," he says. "Not by a long chalk they ain't. Just mugs, some of 'em are, same as I was."

He took another drink.

"Reckon I must of been a bit looney over 'er," he goes on. "She was a good looker, though, an' a lot of fellers was after 'er. She was the sort that likes to play one feller off against the other — you know the sort. Never 'appy without she's makin' some bloke jealous, see?

"But I was dead nuts on 'er and wanted to get spliced up, so she led me up the garden path proper. Quids I spent on 'er. I 'ad a good job down at ——'s (he named a factory beside the Thames at Hammersmith, which I know well). Four quid a week with overtime. I tell yer, I was all right. Put a few quid by, too, so we could get spliced proper.

"Then one day, wivout a word ter me, she goes off and gets spliced to a chap what'd been one o' my mates at the works. Talk abaht mad! — yer wouldn't believe. After all I spent on 'er, too.

"Well, I goes out an' 'as a good blind, same as you might, and when I sees this bloke again I bashes 'im good and proper. 'E 'ad to go to 'ospital with 'is arm broke. I'd 'a bashed 'er, too, if I'd seen 'er again. There was a blow-up at the works, o' course, an' I gets the push. An' 'ere I am."

The speech of Harry Trussler, now in the middle

of his fourth earthquake is growing slightly blurred, and his gestures have the elaborate slowness of a man who is becoming a little drunk.

"But what *brought* you here?" I ask.

"Couldn't get a job. I 'ad a few quid, an' I was bluin' it in, getting blind-o. I met a bloke in a pub who talked a lot about the Legion, said 'e wanted to join, so what abaht us joinin' together. Sounded all right to me, being one over the eight, so next day we takes a coupler week-end tickets to Boulogne an' joins up at the first recruiting office."

"Sounds easy enough."

"Not so easy when you get to Sidi-bel-Abbes (the Algerian training depot). Blimy, they don't 'arf keep you on the 'op. Breakin' you in, like."

We sit for a long while listening to Harry Trussler's reminiscences. They cover a variety of subjects, from the good old times he used to have in London to adventures he has had with certain "tow-haired bits" who are the camp followers of the French army in Morocco. He is becoming more than a little drunk, but he is enjoying himself.

We begin to consider the advisability of leaving when the unexpected happens.

A Legionnaire who has just entered passes our table, catches sight of Harry Trussler, and makes some jeering comment in French, the import of which we cannot catch. It seems that there is hostility between the pair. Trussler's eyes and mouth turn suddenly vicious.

Then he picks up an empty glass and flings it savagely at the other.

Fortunately it misses the man's head and crashes in pieces against the wall beyond. There is a sudden hush in the café; the card games are suspended; the waiter hurries forward. The tormentor throws another gibe at Trussler, who rises unsteadily to his feet.

And here the Spirit takes a hand. She rises also, faces Harry, and with an appealing expression in her face says:

"*Please*, Harry Trussler, not while I'm here. Will you take me out before you deal with him?"

She knows the art of humouring an intoxicated man. For a moment Harry is mollified. Swaying a little on his feet, he crooks his arm in an elaborate gesture, and with a solemnity born of drunkenness says:

"'S all ri', lady, I'll take care o' you. Shafe enough with 'Arry Trussler. No place for a lady."

She takes his arm and together they walk to the door. I following. Outside, with the icy night wind blowing down on us in the white dusty square, Harry stands swaying a little.

"Now I mus' go back an' bash 'em," he says huskily.

The Spirit faces up to him again.

"Now, Harry Trussler," she says. "You're an Englishman and a Londoner, as we are. *Don't* tell me you are going to let yourself be upset by that *scum*. Why, they're beneath your notice."

Harry stares solemnly as the words penetrate through some crevice of his earthquake-shattered mind.

"Shcum," he repeats softly, "'As right . . . shcum . . . You calls 'em shcum . . . I calls 'em shcum" — he waved his hand in a slow comprehensive gesture that included all the universe — 'we all calls 'em shcum . . . So they mus' be shcum!"

"Rotten scum," I add.

"*Bloody* rotten shcum," insists Harry, determined to have the final choice of adjectives.

We ask him to show us the barracks where he lives — so that we can get him home. He is as docile now as a stroked cat by the fire. We feel responsible for him, since his state is due to our entertainment, and we cannot leave him to get into trouble. Arm in arm the three of us walk the short distance to the barracks.

Harry begins to sing a maudlin song that reminds us of homegoing Cockneys on a Bank Holiday night. Once he stops, breaks into a shrill laugh, and in the surprised tone of one who has made a stupendous discovery, says, " *Shcum* ! Tha's what my ole ma used to fling away when she made 'er jam."

We leave him safely inside the barracks gateway, and, departing after an orgy of handshakes, take with us his reiterated assurance that we are two of the best ruddy pals he has ever run acrost . . .

So ends our first encounter with the famous Foreign Legion.

Now I do not wish you to regard our experience as a confirmation of all the stories you may have heard or read to the detriment of this much-maligned corps. Most of them are untrue, many are grossly exaggerated. Usually they are told by men who, in the words of Legionnaire Harry Trussler, couldn't "take it," managed to escape, and for popular newspaper consumption magnified the details of what is normally a hard, strictly-disciplined life, with normal punishments for disobedience, into a tale of horror and cruelty.

As later I was to discover for myself, the Legion is a regiment with a great tradition, of which the best of its members — men who have re-enlisted after their initial five years and given all their lives to its service — are not a little proud. Honour and Fidelity is its motto, courage and determination two of its chief characteristics. To the Legion France owes more than to any other of her regiments the conquest of her colonial empire; and France has not been slow to acknowledge the debt.

In a corps composed of so strange and mixed a

collection of men, strict discipline is essential. There are forty-eight nationalities in the Legion. Of these French and Belgian predominate, making nearly forty per cent of the total. Thirty per cent are German. Then there are Italians and Czechs and Poles and Hungarians, Dutchmen and Danes, Mexicans and Maltese, Russians and Roumanians, Persians and Peruvians, Americans, Canadians and English. A few have been in prison, the majority have not. Some have joined to escape prison, some to escape nagging wives, or the consequences of complications with women; others because they were weary of the monotony of life in office or shop, and sought adventure; or because there was no employment for them in their own countries; or because they just wanted to " see what it was like."

The best soldiers in the Legion's ranks are the Germans and the French, who belong to military nations; the worst are the English, because they do not take kindly to discipline and are not, like most continental people, "good mixers" among other nationalities.

These men join for a minimum of five years. They receive a bonus of about five pounds on enlistment, further bonuses on top of their average pay of about four francs a day, an annual three weeks leave which they can spend in holiday houses in Rabat or Meknes, and are repatriated with further bonus when they finish their service. If they re-enlist and remain in the Legion for fifteen years, they are granted a useful pension and assisted to find employment when they leave.

You will realise that men who have been accustomed to the life of the towns and cities of the world miss its distractions and amenities in this hard life in the lonely places. So what should a man do, when he has the chance, but drink and forget? Women and drink are the hobbies of the Legionnaires. On pay nights ninety per cent of the men set out to have one glorious binge. If there is money left, they have another on the next night. The rest of the fortnight they are a sober and hard-working labour corps.

Please do not, then, blame our friend Harry Trussler for his hour of relaxation and forgetfulness. Do not grudge him the headache to which he assuredly awakened next morning. You or I, in Harry's place, might experience many such a head. Some of us, indeed, have done so, without the justification of Harry's memories and tribulations.

4

When I went to the Spirit's room in the morning I asked her how she had enjoyed the bed of the Gay Lady.

"The most comfortable bed I have slept in since I left home," she assured me. "And the warmest" . . .

We need all the warmth we can find this morning, for the weather is colder and brighter than ever. Even my overcoat is not proof against the icy wind from Ayachi, so that I am compelled to go in quest of a muffler in one of the small ramshackle shops in the square. I find a good thick woolly affair for ten francs, or about one and threepence, wind it round my neck, and am ready for a day's exploring.

From the hill on which Midelt stands we can see for many miles across the plain. At intervals amid the barren lands stand great yellow *ksour* (the plural of *ksar*), mud-walled villages of the Saharan regions. They look like mediaeval fortresses, built to resist the assault of invading hordes; yet a shell or two from a modern gun would reduce them in a few minutes to powder. For centuries they have been the homes of clans of the Berber tribe of Ouled Ait Isdeg, Sons of the Child of Isdeg.

We walk through the town towards the nearest *ksar*. On the way the only people we meet are natives and soldiers: men of the Air Force, black troops of the Sultan, Berber levies, Foreign Legionnaires, and occasionally a picturesque *mokhazni* in flowing pale blue cloak and white turban. These men form a kind of native *gendarmerie*, assisting the French Intelligence Service. They are magnificent fellows, chosen for their skill as fighters and their knowledge of the native ways and dialects.

Soon we come in sight of a mountain stream that runs near the *ksar*. In the distance we can see people along its banks performing a strange kind of dance. They are leaping, they are hopping, they are stamping, first on one foot, then on the other, sometimes on both. We suspect we are witnessing some strange rites, perhaps the appeasement of an evil *djinn* of the river.

But no. It is merely washing day. The dancers are jumping on clothes which they have removed from their bodies and deposited on flat stones at the river's edge. We stay to watch them a while; the Spirit sketches their antics. One of the most vigorous washers is an old white-bearded Berber, who seems determined that no vestige of uncleanliness shall remain in his garments. You might suspect that he had a grudge against them, so savage is his assault. His bony legs leap to a definite rhythm of *one-two, one*; *one-two, one*. A small boy sits near, beating out the rhythm on a pottery drum. The old man leaps and pounds and splashes, pausing presently to examine the enemy with critical eye; then continues the attack, keeping perfect time to the drum.

The women washers are no less vigorous, but they are not so spectacular in their style as this old man. They content themselves with a kind of "marking time" on their clothes, as though they were waiting for an order to "quick march" which never comes. And while they mark time they discuss this and that with each other, or argue shrilly with a neighbour, which seems to be the way of all washerwomen.

Several women look at the Spirit in a manner that reminds us of nervous animals, and as we pass they raise a hand with fingers spread between themselves and her. It is the sign of the hand of Fatima, given to ward off the evil eye. It is directed always at the Spirit, not at me; and we are puzzled to know why she in particular should be credited with the power of evil . . .

Later, when we made enquiries, we were told that her red hair was the cause. Among the Children of Isdeg there is a superstition that red hair brings bad luck. Nobody knows the origin of the belief; doubtless it began when some red-haired woman wrought evil on her neighbours and so gave the colour a bad name. Yet it is curious, as the Spirit points out, that red hair should always be suspect. Invariably it is the badge of the woman spy of chromatic fiction. Men usually suspect a red-haired woman of the worst, women mistrust her. She is supposed to have a temper, she is believed to be a vamp, and she is always perilous to men.

In blissful ignorance of the effect of red hair, we wander on until we come to a garden where fig trees and tamarind grow in the shade of ancient olive groves, and the red hibiscus burns amid silver-green foliage. Sultans of old walked under these trees in the days of the great dynasties; and not far away lies Kasabi, once their stronghold but now a garrison for the dark-skinned troops of the Sultan of to-day, who is no more than a vassal of France.

While we were examining the trees and flowers an ancient man seated on an incredibly small donkey drew up and addressed us affably but incomprehensibly.

We replied with salutations in French and English, but it was all the same to him; he understood no word of ours, nor we of his. But he saw our interest in the flowers and began to tell us about them, pointing out this and that, and pulling down branches for us to examine. We appreciated his kindness and made a great show of understanding his lesson in botany. For ten minutes he talked; then he shook hands and clattered away, delivering many a loud whack on the rump of his donkey . . .

There is gaiety this evening at the restaurant opposite our lodging. The orchestra of three has a greater air of cheerfulness, for it has dined and wined, sitting at a table near us, and there is now a zest in its playing. And when we too have dined and wined, we decide that it would look churlish to stay aloof, since everybody else takes the floor, so we join in a fox-trot. Most of the dancers are French officers and non-commissioned officers, and the barmaids are in great demand, for there is a distressing scarcity of feminine partners. Several of the officers have brought girls with them: the ubiquitous blonde is much in evidence.

The fact that we are not aloof but show an inclination to mix and be happy encourages a young German corporal of the Legion to approach the Spirit and ask for a dance. His daring is watched by the young officers, who perhaps had not the social courage to make the approach: they are expecting him to receive a snub. I think they are a little chagrined to see that this despised Legionnaire should have stepped in where officers of more reputable regiments fear to tread. But this young corporal has established a precedent, and for the rest of the evening the Spirit has no peace, but must give a dance to every man who asks. As for me, I console myself with the barmaids, who as we dance regale me with small-talk about the people of the town.

And when presently we are in a merry group together, and the wine at fourpence a bottle is flowing, we discover that we are the hero and heroine of a desperate affair that occurred at the Café Occidental the previous night. It appears that a fight broke out between Legionnaires. It seems that we took sides with a Legionnaire who was our friend; we had come all the way from London to see him. He was in fact my brother. Apparently in defending this brother of mine I had sailed in and knocked out two other Legionnaires. I was, in fact, a hell of a fighter, a big blonde fellow, and I was on the verge of wrecking the place when my red-haired companion intervened, harangued the men, stopped the fight, and bought drinks all round.

It was a fantastic version of our adventure with Harry Trussler of Hammersmith. It was also evidence of the heights to which imagination will carry the men of the Legion. Perhaps in the course of time this story will have grown into local legend worthy to rank with the romance of Jack the Giant Killer, with the addition of a Jill.

It is midnight before we leave the restaurant. A dozen of our new companions accompany us across the road to the hotel door, and there is a great orgy of handshaking and farewells, for in the morning we pass on.

We creep into our chilly beds warm with a glow of good companionship and bad wine. I think I am a little, just a little intoxicated. Forgive me — but it was such a happy evening . . .

In the morning, when madame brings in our coffee and rolls, she tells us that the *locataire* of the Spirit's room is returning. As we are leaving by the bus at mid-day, would we be so kind as to remove the Spirit's belongings into my room, so that the *locataire* can take possession?

But certainly, with pleasure, madame.

When we have packed and are leaving the hotel for our last excursion in Midelt — the Spirit is to spend the morning painting the exquisite white Catholic church on the edge of the plain — we pass in the corridor a little elderly spinsterish woman who acknowledges us with a slight bow and a prim smile before she enters the room of the Gay Lady. She carries a small valise.

We look in at the office at the end of the corridor and ask madame if that was the *locataire*.

Yes, says madame, she has returned from a visit to Meknes.

But, we ask, puzzled, — that room — that is not her taste?

Mais oui, says madame, with a shrug and a smile, *c'est son goût*.

She tells us that the *locataire* has a nephew in the Legion. He is her only relative, and she likes to be near him. Where he is stationed, there she goes to stay. They are Germans. It is sad. But the Legion is like that. There are many mysteries in the Legion.

When we are outside the Spirit says, "Now I wonder what pathetic story of repression lies behind that queer room?"

I wonder, too. But we shall never know.

CHAPTER 7.

Tells of a Journey through Fantasy — Pram in the Wilderness — Shy Savage, or the Girl who Carved Up Men — Some Queer Hotels — Snow White's Stepmother — the Greek and the Lady — Bungalow Paradise — the Whispering Gnome — Whirlwind — Mud Village of Secrets — a Saint at Home — Bribery for a Holy Man — Café Chantant.

I

Ksar es Souk is our next place of call. The name has an exciting sound, for it brings visions of the hot south and the desert: Ksar es Souk, the Village of the Market, an oasis on the route to the Sahara.

The bus that is to take us from Midelt gives proof of the roughness of the journey, for it is rather a battered affair; it rattles inordinately, and most of its windows, which need to be closed to keep out the cold air, persist in sliding open, so that the passengers who sit next to them must perpetually hold them firm.

Our companions now are soldiers and officers; we are the only civilians. The back section of this well-worn bus is divided off by a wood and glass partition into a second-class compartment, which is crowded with Berbers and Arabs. At the beginning of the journey a little conversation passes between us, but soon the rattle and drone of the bus and the heat of its interior sets the soldiers nodding to sleep. To them the trip is no adventure, it is part of the routine of their lives; but to us there is so much to interest in passing that I think we could stay awake even if the atmosphere were charged with chloroform.

The road passes at first across the level yellow plain; but soon we begin to mount the lower slopes of the Grand Atlas chain, where in the distance white-capped Ayachi still towers into the intense blue sky.

Again we are in the cedar forests, passing through great gorges where shining streams pour out of the rocky places and shatter themselves a hundred feet below into rainbows of spray in the sunshine. Sometimes we are on top of the world, creeping along a perilous ledge of a road that runs round silver-grey peaks from which we look down on a wilderness of lesser peaks; sometimes we plunge into a gorge where the heights threaten to overwhelm us. The white road twists and wriggles, turns back on itself, leaps over mountains, dives into culverts, sneaks furtively round unsuspected corners.

Presently we emerge into a country of barren mountains and hills of fantastic form and incredible colour; hills that change from magenta to rose, from purple to terracotta, in the shape of pudding-basins, sugar-cones, half oranges, French loaves stood on end. Mountainsides are built in strata patterns that resemble the coloured layers of a Russian cake. Never have we seen such incredible rock formations, such fantasies of colouring.

Then, ahead of us on this tortured road, we approach a long low tunnel cut through the side of a round terracotta mountain. Before we pass through the bus stops to fill up with petrol, and we have a few minutes to spare for exploration.

Now this tunnel is a very famous one. Above its entrance is an inscription: "The mountain barred the way; the order was given to pass; the Legion carried out the order."

At the other end is another inscription: "The strength of their muscles and the determination of their will were their only instruments."

Here, for those who want it, is an everlasting

monument to the Foreign Legion, whose men only a few years ago created this stupendous road through these mountains of fantasy. Here, too, is something that explains why the Legion is no place for weaklings.

Once through this tunnel, we know that we have reached the south. The burning sunshine suggests it, the dry heat of the air emphasises it, the panorama of the country proves it. We are on a ledge three hundred feet up the sides of a gorge. Far below the river Ziz lies like an emerald serpent between rose-coloured cliffs and mountains. Clusters of tall date palms dream beside its silver-blue shores, where a great *ksar* of yellow mud stands like a fortress guarding its precious waters.

We are descending rapidly now, and soon we have left the oasis on our right and pass between ranges of pale rose hills across a wilderness of ochre and grey stone. The only vegetation here is a small dusty grey scrub which looks as though it has lived without water since birth.

Looking ahead on this rough track across the uninhabited wilderness, we see something that makes us wonder if our eyes are deceiving us. A dapper little man in civilian clothes is calmly pushing an elegant pram, in which lies a pink-faced baby. Beside him strolls his wife, well-dressed in a neat tailor-made. So incongruous is this sight in the sun-stricken desolation of the plain that we break into involuntary laughter.

The little man turns as we rattle towards him, answers the salute which our driver waves to him, and continues his perambulation.

And now a few flat yellow houses rise out of the plain. The first of them proves to be the Hotel Continental; the name is painted across its dilapidated façade. It is a square, flat-roofed bungalow; its door has fallen off and its windows are glassless holes; it is a ruin, the relic of some Frenchman's misguided enterprise. A few hundred yards more, and we pass through a forest of barbed-wire entanglements into Rich, a military post beside the *ksar* inhabited by clans of our friends the Children of Isdeg.

This barbed wire tells its own story; we have reached the edge of the region where four years ago the Berbers put up their last fight for independence. Some hundred yards behind the barbed wire lies the military stronghold, a long, fortress-like compound bounded by red crenelated walls twelve feet high, in which at intervals rise square observation towers.

Here we stay for a time, while the driver delivers mail and despatches to a young Legionnaire who has the face of a poet and the smile of a saint. We would like to talk to him, but he has gone about his business before we can take the opportunity. So we sit in the hot sunshine and talk instead to one of our fellow travellers, a French *sous* officer of the same regiment. He tells us that four years ago he was fighting the Berbers not forty miles from here, in the region of Mount Baddou; hard and dangerous times they were, he says, hemming in these tribesmen in their mountain fastness, cutting them off from their water supplies, driving them into the caves and passes of their rock-bound world until their only alternative to starvation and death was surrender.

A young Berber woman approaches, offering a small bunch of flowers for sale. Heaven knows where she finds them in this barren wilderness; perhaps down on the banks of the Ziz not far away. She is a fine-looking girl, and there is an attractive shyness in her manner and her smile. Our sergeant knows her well, and greets her with some jest in her own tongue.

When we remark on her good looks and gentle manner, he laughs. There was a time, he says, when we would have held a different opinion as to her gentleness. She comes from the region of Mount

Baddou, and she took part in the fighting not so long ago. Her business, like that of all the Berber women in battle, was to urge on their men from the rear and look after the captives and wounded. Her attentions consisted either of slitting their throats or torturing them. One method of finishing off a wounded prisoner was to cut open his stomach and fill it with glowing charcoal; and it had been this young woman's claim after the war that she had served eight Legionnaires in this way.

Yet she is friendly enough now, he says; an attractive woman with whom a good many of the men would like to have an *affaire* if she were not so faithful to her husband.

But would they, the Spirit asks, feel quite happy in having an *affaire* with a woman who was capable at any moment of carving them up and making an oven of their insides?

The sergeant laughed. That would add to the thrill, he intimated. Life was dull enough in these days for men out here; the spice of a little danger in love would be welcome. That was the one thing the Legion lacked now — excitement. They couldn't find any. Even the subdued Berbers were peaceful and bore their conquerors no resentment. When the Berbers were successful in war, they knew that Allah was with them; but when they were beaten, then Allah so willed it. A Berber respected those who had the backing of Allah. Yet any reverse for the French, any weakness, would mean that Allah had turned against them, . . . *voilà*. He drew his finger across his throat. This fatalism of the North Africans, he said, was an asset to the French — so long as the Berbers thought that Allah had decreed that the French should be the victors . . .

Our bus driver calls us with a clamour from his horn and we are off again, across the yellow stony plain through the rose-brown hills, swaying and bumping on a rough track to which we have been diverted by repairs which gangs of Berbers are making to the road. A mile or two from Rich the driver pulls up suddenly and points ahead, and there is a general slamming of windows. Through the valley we see advancing towards us a yellow cloud, which leaps over the little hills and races down their sides in a panic hurry to reach us. In a few seconds we are enveloped in it, a swirling blast of yellow dust like a London fog. No windows are proof against its pervasiveness. Through unsuspected crevices and unseen holes in the well-worn bus it spurts in little jets like yellow steam, blinding us, setting us coughing, and mingling with the perspiration on our faces to form a kind of mud-pack.

For perhaps half a minute we are lost in this dust-storm, stifled in the airless heat of the bus; then as suddenly as it arrived it has passed, and we see it speeding far away through the hills behind us. When the windows are flung open and we are on our way again, the wind created by our speed is like a cooling drink.

We follow now the valley of the Ziz, which runs through this rocky wilderness carrying life to the desert. Sometimes we pass a Berber settlement, one of the great mud *ksour*, set in a cluster of palm trees beside the blue water; and there are pathetically small patches of cultivated land where grain grows, irrigated by channels cut in the burnt-up yellow soil into which water is poured from the river. And presently we see before us, on a long low hill in the plain, a small town of red flat-roofed houses set in blocks intersected by wide roadways. Wandering beside it is the shining river on whose banks are many of these great Berber fortress-villages, set amid palm groves that mark the course of the Ziz; and around all this a distant circle of mauve and rose hills encloses Ksar es Souk in a world of its own.

2

The bus deposits us with our scanty pieces of luggage, which included "The Body," in a wide square like a parade ground. On one side is the long red wall of the military post; on the other the square red mud bungalows of the town, each with a kind of colonnade of Moorish archways also built of mud.

It is tea-time, we are hungry, since we have eaten nothing except apples and dates since morning; we are also dusty and thirsty and tired, and we need an hotel.

Our Legion sergeant points out two buildings among the red bungalows and says they are hotels. There is another, he says, it is a long way off, but it is the same as these; there is not much to choose between them.

So we try the first. We are received by an old woman who is lame, who has the face of a witch and the eye of an hawk. If you have seen the film Snow White and remember the aspect of the stepmother Queen, when she changed herself into an old woman, you have a good caricature of this landlady. Oh, yes, she has rooms, splendid rooms, so clean, so cheap, the best rooms in Ksar es Souk, she says, as she hobbles round with us to prove her claim.

Now this is a very queer sort of hotel. Its rooms are on the outside, opening on to the street, and there is no communication with the interior of the house. They look clean, it is true, with their bare cement floors and iron bedsteads; but they do not appeal to the Spirit.

"Anybody could break in at night," she says. "There would be no escape and no one to come to one's help."

We ask Snow White's stepmother if she has any rooms inside the house. Yes, yes, such good rooms inside, splendid rooms. We follow her into a narrow court where we disturb multitudes of flies enjoying a full dustbin, and enter another chamber. It has no window, is below ground, and has an earth floor. In one corner is a padlocked door, beneath an opening two feet square covered with wire netting, beyond which is darkness.

"What's in there?" asked the Spirit.

"Nothing, nothing, madame," says the old woman. "Just a store-room."

"You mean you have to go there to get stores when I may be in bed?"

"No, no, no, no, madame, but of course not. Only when you are not there."

This was too much for the Spirit. Although she was prepared to live rough, she could not face the prospect of sleeping in a dark windowless chamber that was part of a store, in which might lurk all manner of strange things. So we told the witch that we would like to look round the town before deciding on a room.

At once her ingratiating smile vanished, her long mouth set in a hard thin line, and she stumped away into the recesses of the building, leaving us there with the luggage.

"We'll try the next," says the Spirit.

A negro boy in a tattered shirt and without trousers carries our luggage towards the next block. On the way we meet a young Greek with a fine aquiline nose, black curling hair and a glistening pair of eyes, who looks at us eagerly as though he would like to speak.

"Could you tell us," the Spirit asks him, "which is the best hotel in the town?"

He indicates the next red mud building.

"This is the best," he says. "It is mine."

We go to inspect, doubting. Across the verandah we step through a pair of glass-panelled doors into a dusty concrete-paved corridor open to the sky. On either side are ranged eight rooms. At the end of the corridor is a cabin with a hole in the ground which serves as the lavatory, from which comes an effluvia that catches the breath.

We look at the rooms. They are an improvement on those of Snow White's stepmother, for each has a window and there are pieces of dusty matting beside the iron beds on the cement floor.

We discuss whether we should take rooms here. The sun is near the horizon, darkness falls swiftly in these regions, and we do not wish to be stranded roomless in a strange town which has no street lighting. So we decide to book here at least for the night and hope for something more comfortable in the morning; though we doubt whether there is likely to be anything better in this desert town.

Another bed has to be brought into our room. The Greek and his negro doorkeeper fetch an enormous double affair from another room, with much jangling and scraping of iron on the concrete floor. Apparently it cannot be taken to pieces; yet somehow they manage to edge it through the door, and by the time it is in the room there is scarcely space for us to turn.

While this manoeuvring is going on, a young woman in a purple dressing gown comes to the door of a room opposite and watches us with frank curiosity. She leans negligently against her doorpost. She has long peroxide curls, very red lips, and she is ample in her proportions. Behind her in the room we glimpse a bed covered with a purple bedspread, yellow and blue rugs on the stone floor, pink curtains at the window.

" I think," says the Spirit, " there can be no doubt about it this time. But . . . I do hope she doesn't think I am a rival."

When the business of settling in has finished, we ask the Greek where we can eat. There is the café in the square, he says, which belongs to the old woman; or there is the other hotel, the Roi de la Bière, which is about two hundred metres away. Since the old woman was so clearly offended by us, we have no alternative but to choose the other hotel.

We find it after a short walk through the wide rough roadways between the red boxes that are houses, at whose doors Berber women sit idling or doing their various jobs of embroidering and sewing. It is a square red box, like all the rest, facing a dusty road beyond which lies the desert of brown rock that reaches to the horizon.

Entering the narrow door, we expect to find conditions no better than in the two other hotels. Instead, we are in a passage where we tread on polished brown and white tiles, between walls distempered a pale grey. At the end of this passage, beyond two Moorish arches, there is a hall, tiled and white-walled, wherein are set half a dozen tables covered with snowy cloths and laid with shining silver. So exquisitely clean and bright and cool is this mud hotel that the Spirit exclaims aloud; she says she feels she has found a diamond in a dustheap.

A grave young Berber in a white jacket and apron greets us. We ask if we can get tea, and in a few minutes he has brought it, with milk and sweet biscuits and jam and butter — the best tea we have had since we left home.

The Spirit leans back in her comfortable chair with a sigh and prepares to enjoy herself.

" This is clearly the Ritz of Ksar es Souk," she

says. "And this is where we must stay. I feel we can be happy here."

I agree, for there is a friendly intimacy about this little inn, and a quiet beauty which we had not hoped to find after our experiences at the other hotels.

"But what shall we do about the Greek?" she adds.

"Pay him off and get the luggage."

"You don't think he'll be unpleasant?"

"I don't mind if he is. I would face any number of unpleasant Greeks after this cup of tea."

"So would I — especially after this jam."

When we have finished tea we call the Berber waiter and ask about rooms. The tour of inspection on which he takes us is a further proof of what can be done with a mud-built house of the desert. The floor of each room is paved with maroon and white tiles, on which lie black and white Berber rugs. The walls are white, there are wardrobes with mirrors, modern beds, electric light, running water in wall-basins, and curtained off in a corner, the miracle of a shower bath. Small square casement windows that open on to the desert are protected by wrought iron grilles.

Of the five rooms in the hotel, two are vacant, so we engage them. They are connected by a lobby and form almost a suite.

"Isn't it wonderful," exclaims the Spirit, "to have a suite in the wilderness when we might have been sleeping in those terrible places."

And now comes the business of removing our belongings from the possession of the Greek. I ask our Berber if he can send for them, but he explains that it will be necessary for me to go in person, since the Greek might think that a client was being stolen from him.

So while the Spirit is enjoying the luxury of a shower I walk back and explain to the Greek that, pleasant though we find his hotel, I feel that the other would be more suitable for *madame*. He shrugs, spreads his hands in a gesture of resignation, gives me a receipt for the twenty-four francs which is the price of the room for a night — plus two francs forty for service — and hails the negro boy who had been our carrier.

As the luggage is hauled out, the ample blonde emerges from her doorway and calls out something which from the tone of her voice I am sure is not complimentary. In ten minutes we are settled in the suite which is to be our home for a week.

And now it is necessary to make the acquaintance of M. Berujon, the Frenchman who runs this oasis in an oasis. From a room which is his office and bedroom just beyond our suite he pops like a gnome. We find that he has a habit of popping. He emerges from the most unexpected places. He wears baggy white Turkish trousers with pockets braided in black, a yellow canvas jacket, and a brown skull cap on his bald round head. There is a serious and purposeful air about everything he does.

Our first acquaintance with him was when he tapped on our door, put his head round when we called to him to enter, and in a hoarse excited whisper hissed something about "*le police.*"

Startled, we stood staring at him.

"*Police?*" I queried.

"*Police?*" echoed the Spirit.

"*Oui, le police,*" whispered M. Berujon. "*C'est très important.*"

"But what have we to do with the police?" I ask.

Still in that tense whisper, M. Berujon explains. It is necessary that all who come to Ksar es Souk must call at the police office and register.

We are relieved; we feared from M. Berujon's tense whisperings that something sinister and mysterious was in the air. We now discover that M. Berujon whispers because he must; he has permanently lost his voice. You will understand that at first we find his manner of speech disconcerting; it invests everything he says with a thrilling secrecy. And it is infectious. Once later on, in a moment of mental aberration, I caught myself whispering back at him, as though we were sharing a secret which nobody else must overhear.

We soon grow to love M. Berujon, with his serious, rather worried looking face and his perpetual poppings here and everywhere. He is always busy. Sometimes he pops to the kitchen to superintend the dinner he has prepared with his own hands and left in charge of two negro assistants; sometimes to his office to attend to accounts, or to the white hall to see that the tables are well prepared.

He is proud of his kitchen. He takes us round to show us the fine range where he cooks the meals in shining copper pans over glowing charcoal. He shows us in the courtyard the small engine with which he makes his own electric light. He leads us to the *cabinet de toilette*, flings open the door, and reveals a tiled white interior with a modern lavatory and flush; and it seems that he lingers here, expecting us to pay special homage.

" *C'est très gentil*," says the Spirit.

" *C'est magnifique*," says I. " *Très rare*."

"It is the only one in the town," M. Berujon confides in a hoarse whisper.

Now until you have travelled through these regions, you will perhaps not appreciate the significance of his prideful gesture. The *cabinets de toilette* of the south are foul and dangerous places, mere holes in the ground, the breeding places for flies and all manner of germs. To have achieved a modern contraption is indeed a matter for pride.

We observe later that M. Berujon inspects this treasure of his a dozen times a day. He guards it jealously. Whenever his ears tell him that it has been in use, he comes out of his room to see who the user may be, so that if it has not been treated as a modern lavatory should be treated, he will know on whom to lay the blame. He has it washed out many times a day. There is nothing he will not do to preserve and protect this unique possession.

He takes a pride, too, in his cuisine. We see him presently making great preparations at a table, attended by his kitchen assistants; and soon an exceedingly good odour permeates the bungalow. Purposeful footsteps sound in the tiled corridor beside our rooms, becoming increasingly frequent; and there is a noise of laughter and many voices as though somebody is giving a party.

When we go out to the hall we find the tables occupied by a score of youthful officers from the camp; their black and red caps hang in rows on pegs in the corridor. A priest enters, passing to another room where there is also a sound of voices and much laughter.

Our Whispering Gnome evidently knows the secret of making men happy with good food and wine; hence he draws all the custom of the camp. Here are flying men who day by day soar over the Atlas and the desert, keeping a watchful eye on the doings of the tribes, and infantry officers, engineers, lieutenants of the Legion, even privates — all come to spend some or all of their week's pay on one of M. Berujon's dinners. Most of them, we learn later, have *en pension* terms for meals at reduced rate; so that M. Berujon can afford to serve up a good dinner every night without fear that it will be wasted through lack of customers.

And what a dinner he serves in this mud bungalow by the desert. Under the soft glow of shaded electric lights, fed by the engine which we can hear faintly throbbing out in the yard, we eat as we might in London or Paris. Here is the menu:

Consommé

Filet de Truite Sidi Ali

Poulet de Grain en Cocotte

Haricots Verts

Cotelettes de Veau Zerhoun

Pommes Mignonettes

Caramel Ziz   Fruits Variés

Café

Prix 20 francs.   Vin non Compris.

At half a crown we consider this dinner a miracle. We are on the edge of the wilderness, in an oasis where little grows except palm trees and the scanty grain of the native allotments. Transport is scarce and difficult. Cooking is done over charcoal, which has to be constantly fanned to keep it aglow. And the heat of the region, set in a plain amid arid hills, is enough to turn the freshest of food bad in a day. Yet M. Berujon achieves such a dinner as this every evening.

There is one defect: the meat is tough. But that is not entirely the fault of M. Berujon. There is little green pasture for cattle and the climate makes it necessary for meat to come straight from the slaughter house to the table. The further south we travel the tougher becomes the meat. Yet it would be possible to have tender beef if only the French would take a lesson in cooking from the Arabs instead of so obstinately preserving their national methods of preparation. This meat is suitable not for quick grilling, but for long slow roasting and stewing. Not once in an Arab meal have we encountered tough meat; not once in a French meal have we had it tender.

But it would be churlish to criticise M. Berujon, since he has done us so well in other respects. His trout from the lake of Sidi Ali, far away in the mountains near Azrou, is perfection; his chicken and beans, which he brings from the north, could not be improved upon; and his caramel has a delicacy of flavour that would give satisfaction even to Marcel Boulestin. As for the coffee — well, M. Berujon is a Frenchman.

When we have finished, and the crowd of guests at his party have gone back to their quarters, we go outside to sample the night. The small town is in darkness, though it is only nine o'clock. Above, the stars are brilliant like diamonds, large as Koh-i-noors; and before us lies the black void of the wilderness, whence comes from the distance a strange chinking sound, half-metallic, half-musical, as though someone were rattling many coins in a glass jar.

We listen awhile, and realise at last that we are hearing the mating call of a multitude of frogs down on the bank of the Ziz. Presently even this ceases, and the desert silence falls on Ksar es Souk; so intense, so suggestive of death and oblivion, that we shiver and creep back to M. Berujon's bungalow, grateful for its soft lights and the sounds of life from its kitchen.

At ten o'clock the engine in the yard suddenly ceases to throb, and by the light of candles we go to bed, leaving M. Berujon's negro custodian curled up in a red rug against the front door, where he lies on guard till morning.

3

At six a.m. I was awakened by a curious whining sound outside my window, and lay for a minute trying to decide what it might be. There was something in the sound that suggested the human voice, and there was something, too, that made me think of cats.

I got out of bed and threw back the wooden shutters; and there, looking at me through the window, which is no more than four feet above the rough roadway, was a group of tattered Arab children, holding out their hands and begging for anything I might be disposed to give away. Their small dark faces are set in expressions of such anguished despair, their wailing voices are so full of hopeless misery, that I burst into a laugh; whereupon their wailing becomes shriller and more intense, for they know that my laughter is friendly. They know, too, that when the guests at this house rise in the morning they are served in their rooms with coffee and crisp fresh brioche and butter, and that some of this is likely to come the way of him who wails long and loud enough.

So when our waiter, whose name is Ali, brings in our trays, we liven the *petit déjeuner* by tossing buttered scraps from the window and watching the scramble that follows.

When at seven o'clock we go out into the hot sunshine, carrying painting kit — for the Spirit is eager to get something on to her canvas — there is a surge of vivid colourful life on the dusty roadway. White-garbed Arabs, Berbers in their stripes or in rags and tatters, cheerful, noisy negroes, women veiled and unveiled are converging on a great red-walled compound with a high arched entrance that stands on the edge of the brown wilderness a hundred yards from the hotel. It is the *souk*, the market from which Ksar es Souk takes its name. We wander through its bargaining crowds, inspecting the wares. Their quality and kind tell a story of scarcity and poverty. The richest traders seem to be the black-garbed Jews, who occupy small arched alcoves in the walls and display the wares of other people's creation; silks and satins, exquisitely primitive Berber rugs woven by hand and sold for a few dozen francs, shoes, peasant pottery made of rough white clay and decorated with red and black design.

The rest of the compound is occupied by the Berbers and Arabs, who sell the products of their own labours; a gallon of grain, a sticky mass of dates stuffed into a bag of sheepskin, hard lumps of yellow crystal which is rock-salt, the carcase of a goat; all laid out on the ground in the burning sun. They do not necessarily want money for their goods, but will dispose of them by barter. Here is a Berber woman exchanging a few lumps of rock-salt for a small quantity of meat; and here a ragged countryman bargaining for an extra handful of grain for which he will give one of the tall graceful water-pitchers of his own making.

With these people trading is less a matter of getting money than of securing the bare sustenance of life. They have not learned the lesson of the Jews — that it is more profitable to sell the creations of others than one's own.

The people here are darker of hue than any we have yet encountered. In many faces there are the signs of negro blood, for the black man and woman have inter-married extensively with the white in these regions south of the Grand Atlas. Sometimes the combination of Berber and negro produces a face that for all its darkness of skin is nevertheless remarkable for strength and fineness of feature and for the lustre of its dark eyes. And it seems to us that the nearer these people approach to the negro, the happier they are. The happiest people we see are the pure negroes, with their great white grins and their cheerful vociferousness.

We pass through the *souk* and on up the hill into the square where we arrived last night. And here the

Spirit decides to set up her easel and get busy. She has a wonderful prospect before her: the red village with its rough arched colonnades which are the mark of Saharan architecture; the tall date palms drooping over the flat roofs; and away in the distance the mountains that glow with a pale rose light in the sunshine. They are for ever changing, these lovely barren hills; with the passage of the sun the shadows in their hollows merge from pale mauve into purple and on to black; and at their summits the sky begins with a strange electric green before it deepens into full azure.

No sooner is the easel set up than we are the centre of a crowd mainly of Arab and Berber boys. A giant negro in red and blue uniform, holding a posy of flowers in one hand, strolls over from the entrance to the army quarters where he is on guard, gives us a genial grin and a greeting, and gurgles delightedly as he sees the bright paints wriggle like coloured worms from their tubes on to the palette.

The boys watch breathlessly, their mouths agape; they are fascinated by this magic colour that comes from tubes and turns itself into buildings and trees and donkeys under the brush.

The Spirit wants one of the boys, a fantastic brown elf with the inevitable pigtail sprouting from the crown of his head, to pose in her picture; so of course all the rest of them want to pose as well. While I hold them off, she arranges him some distance away, where he stands so rigidly that you would think he had been starched. After much effort we induce him to relax into a natural position; and for half an hour he scarcely blinks an eye, so intent is he on being a good model.

And here I leave the artist at work while I wander off to explore the village, hoping to find some people or scenes that might appeal to the Spirit's artistic enthusiasm. When I returned nearly two hours later

I was in time to see disaster fall upon her.

I was crossing the open space, where she still sat with her spectators, when I heard a commotion behind me. I turned and saw a yellow column of sand and dust spiralling towards me. I was preparing to pull my coat over my head when the column unaccountably changed its direction and made straight towards the Spirit.

The Arab boys saw it approaching, and shouted a warning to her; but before she had time to act it was on her. It tore the canvas from the easel and whirled it high in the air, spinning it like a top. It overturned the light easel and sent the small folding stool clattering across the square. The boys were crouching with backs to the whirlwind, their *djellabs* pulled over their heads; but the Spirit, caught unawares, stood there helpless and blinded, her arms across her eyes.

The whirlwind passed on, paused a moment as though in thought, changed its direction again and darted down one of the wide roadways through the red bungalows. And here it suddenly dropped the whirling canvas, as though after inspection it had decided that the picture was not worth the keeping.

While I sped to assist the Spirit, some of the boys ran to retrieve the canvas. They brought it back ruined. Its wet paint was caked with sand.

The Spirit regarded the wreck of her morning's work with rueful eyes. Suddenly she brightened.

"If I keep it till it's dry, it will make wonderful sandpaper," she says. "Saharan sandpaper."

These impish whirlwinds come upon you frequently in this region. They leap at you round corners in a most startling way, on days when the air is still and hot under the sun. They are like playful human creatures who have become bored with the placidity of life down here, and are determined to have a little diversion. We have seen them eddy across a *souk*, sweeping up everything not too heavy to be carried; tearing down fragile tents and scattering the traders' goods. They are splendid fun, these infant whirlwinds, so long as they play their jokes on others than oneself.

This whirlwind was not the only adventure that befell the Spirit that morning while she was painting. During my absence she had other spectators than Arab boys, she tells me. First came a young German of the Foreign Legion, who admired her picture, saying he would like to buy it.

"How much would it be?" he asked.

"Oh, say five hundred francs," said the Spirit.

"Impossible," said the Legionnaire, "I could never afford that. You must be a very famous artist to be able to charge so much."

"That isn't much."

"It is a great deal, as we know money."

Then he transferred his interest from the art to the artist.

"If you are staying here, I would like to meet you in the evening," he said solemnly.

"What does one do in the evening?"

"Go out somewhere."

"Where does one go?"

"Well — just out."

"Cinema?"

"There is no cinema."

"Theatre?"

"There is no theatre either. There is nothing."

"Then where does one go? A walk?"

"There is nowhere to walk, except the desert and the oasis."

Then he brightened.

"We have the café. We sing there sometimes in the evening."

"That sounds fun."

" Then will you come with me to the café ?"

" I'll ask my husband."

" Oh, you have a husband."

" Of course."

" I hadn't thought of that. Then it is no use asking you."

" But we like singing in cafés."

The *tête-à-tête* was interrupted at this point, says the Spirit, by two officers who approached to inspect the picture. They gave a curt order to the Legionnaire and drove him away.

" I hope I shall see you at the café," was the poor fellow's parting word . . .

Since the whirlwind has put an end to the Spirit's artistic enthusiasm for the day, we decide to spend the afternoon in search of new interests. With a picnic lunch of oranges and dates which we buy in a small shop, we set off towards the palm groves beside the Ziz, where the great *ksour* raise their crenelated mud towers and massive walls.

Down the yellow hillside we reach these groves, passing under the shade of date palm and tamarind, where the olive and the fig grow and hibiscus flaunts its crimson glory. Multitudes of blue-backed swallows with white tails flit through the trees, flying close to the ground and coming so near to us that we could catch them with our hands. Our path takes us through the groves along the thirty-feet high yellow cliff beside the shallow river, whose lovely pale jade and blue waters ripple over a wide bed of stones of a whiteness that dazzles in the burning sun. Away on the far side of the Ziz this white shore stretches to the ochre wilderness, and beyond crouch the ranges of low purple hills.

We pass through patches of wheat and maize growing sparsely in sun-dried yellow earth; and sometimes we meet a Berber or an Arab from the *ksar* who breaks off his job of watering his patch to give us a greeting. It is a laborious business, this agriculture, for he must climb down the gulleys in the cliff to fetch water by the bucketful; but happily these people know nothing of the amenities of modern agriculture to make them dissatisfied with their own methods. Their land is allotted to them by grace of the Sultan or the grand Caids of the south; and four-fifths of all they possess goes to the local caid, who retains a part before passing on the remainder to his overlords. The feudal system still lives on among the people of Morocco.

There is the peace of *siesta* down here in the oasis this hot afternoon. The only sound is the faint throbbing of a drum and the high-pitched wail of a singer from among the palms that hide the *ksar* which we are approaching. And presently we come upon it, the first of these villages beside the river, standing like a fortress in a clearing in the grove.

In front of its high arched entrance a crowd of ragged brown children are at play. At first it seems that they are throwing darts or toy aeroplanes, but as we draw nearer we see that their playthings are blue-backed swallows. Some of the children have half a dozen of these lovely birds in their hands. Their game is to tie to the tails a string to which pieces of paper are knotted, like the tail of a kite; then to throw the birds into the air and see how far they can fly.

Usually they cannot get far; after struggling with hard-beating wings for a dozen yards they come thudding to earth, to be thrown up into the air again for another helpless struggle for freedom.

One of them falls at the Spirit's feet. She picks it up and in a burst of compassion pulls the encumbering string from its tail to give it liberty. But the bird can no longer fly; it lies panting in her hand, its limpid brown eyes dazed with pain. She strokes the blue velvet of its back and murmurs her pity over it; and the small brown boy who was its tormentor comes and stands before her, looking into her face with uncomprehending eyes. They have no sense of cruelty, these Berbers and Arabs; pain and suffering in others does not touch them.

The sight of these birds being tortured in play fills us with anger, yet we know we can do nothing about it. The Spirit, still tenderly stroking the dazed swallow, talks to its former tormentor in a tone that would wring pity from stone; but the boy understands neither her words nor her compassion. Her effort to touch his heart with pity is wasted.

"If I can't save them all, at least I can keep this one," she says, and retains it as we walk on.

But the boy follows after us, talking in his own dialect. I gather that we have stolen his bird, so I give him a few centimes and wave him away.

Before we have gone far a dozen children are clamouring round us, holding out hands full of birds. I suggest that we buy and liberate them. So we take the captives from each child in turn, paying a few centimes for them, and release them. The children stare at us in wonder; they cannot understand why we should pay money for something which we throw away.

Around the entrance to the *ksar* the ground is littered with dead bluebirds. As we approach we are greeted by three or four white-bearded elders who sit in the shade of the walls. The massive wooden doors that once guarded the village in the days before the French created law and order are thrown back, falling into dilapidation now that they are no longer needed for protection.

Pausing before the old men, who stare at us with grave solemn eyes, we ask in French if it is permitted to enter. They understand our meaning but not our words, for they answer in their own dialect, and with gestures of their brown bony hands wave us inside. Henceforth they display not the faintest interest in us, but continue their silent contemplation of the outside world.

We enter an open space where a few asses and scraggy horses are tethered before crude mud-built mangers. On the far side two tunnel-like entrances lead into the village, the home of five hundred or more people. We pass into one of these, and immediately we are in darkness. The place is like a rabbit warren. The mud houses of two storeys are built over narrow alleys. Light penetrates only at intervals through small open spaces which the builders have left as by an afterthought between an occasional pair of houses. It is a silent, mysterious world, in which dim figures whose features we cannot see pass noiselessly, startling us by their sudden presence, disappearing into the gloom as uncannily as they emerged.

Curious sounds come from either side of us: faint scrapings, a dull thump, an odd kind of grunt; and our nerves are beginning to fray a little when the reason for these sounds is suddenly made clear by a terrifying, maniacal bellow which deafens and reverberates in the confined space — the braying of a donkey. We realise that the lower parts of these houses are reserved for the animals, while the people live above.

Further on, when we have passed again through a shaft of light into the darkness, we are arrested by a low monotonous growling almost at our feet. We stand, I confess, with heart-beats accelerated and a chilly feeling down the back of our necks. I confess, too, that our instinct was to turn and run. We felt that something was there ready to attack if we moved on; and as we strained our gaze into the darkness we could faintly discern the movement of something greyish on the ground six feet ahead.

I feel the Spirit clutching my arm.

"Shall we go back?" I ask.

"No, it might attack then," she says breathlessly. "Strike a match."

While I am fumbling with the box a voice comes from the moving greyness, speaking an unintelligible language. I strike the match, and there, seated in the dust, is an old man grinding corn. The growling that sent our flesh cold was the sound of his primitive mill: two rough-hewn round stones, one set with a small wooden handle, which he turns to grind his few handfuls of grain . . .

He nods to us, blinking up into the matchlight; and before the faint yellow gleam fades, carrying him into oblivion, we have time to catch the gesture of his hand inviting us to pass. The mumble of his voice and the growl of his millstones follow us.

"I've never been so terrified in my life," says the Spirit.

By the time we have groped our way for sixty yards or so, the shafts of light from above become more frequent, so that we can see around us. At intervals in the rough mud walls there are doors, each of which marks the entrance to a house.

There is no sign of life as we pass these doors; yet once or twice, when we glance behind us, we catch sight of a dim face or two peering out, only to disappear when they see that they have been observed. Although we seem to be alone in this uncanny warren, it is evident that our presence is not passing unobserved.

I stop suddenly and quote:

"Like one who on a lonely road,
Doth walk in fear and dread,
And having once looked round, goes on
And turns no more his head

Because he knows a frightful fiend
Doth close behind him tread."

" I feel rather like that myself," says the Spirit; for
the lines of Coleridge come very near to expressing
our emotions in this strange world of darkness and
silence. We know there is life around us, behind us,
yet it is shy and hidden, reluctant to reveal itself. We
know, too, that we are being followed, not by a
frightful fiend, but by a group of ragged children who
remain at a distance and lurk round corners. When
we pause, they are arrested; when we move on, they
continue the advance.

At last we come to an open space where the full
light of day pours in and the sunlight falls on us like
a blessing. This is evidently a village square. Here
is a little white box-like domed house, tomb of a
marabout or local holy man, before which several
bearded old men sit on their haunches chanting prayers
or asking boons.

In life these *marabouts* have a strong and often
dangerous influence over the tribes. They are credited
with special knowledge bestowed on them by Allah.
They dabble in local politics, and in the bad old
days when clan raided clan they played an important
part in the councils of the elders. They dispensed
propaganda among the warriors, urging them on to
the fight with stories designed to stimulate passions.
I have heard that in the last war with the French, the
tribesmen in the remote places of the High Atlas held
the belief, instilled into them by their *marabouts*, that
enemy soldiers had only one eye each in their fore-
heads, and for food liked nothing better than human
babies eaten half raw. So primitive were these white
savages of the mountains that they believed any
fantasies their holy men cared to tell them.

A young Berber lounging against a doorway gives
us a salute and a "*bonjour*," encouraging us to pause

and talk with him. He is a pleasant fellow, with a slow, quiet smile and light grey eyes. I tell him we find his village very interesting, very picturesque, which pleases him; and when he sees the Spirit peering into the dimness of his home he invites us to enter.

We accept the invitation gladly, and follow him into the lower chamber of his mud house. It measures about fourteen feet by twelve. A donkey and a goat are tethered in separate corners. A mud staircase about two feet wide leads upstairs. Climbing this with difficulty, we find ourselves in another room which has a hard mud floor covered by a coloured rug or two, an opening in one wall which serves as a window, and a rough doorway leading out to a flat roof in the sunshine. The young Berber's wife, a pretty creature in nondescript clothes and with a coloured handker-chief arranged across her dark hair, stands at one side of the room. She is evidently perturbed by this unexpected visit, for she smiles frequently and nervously while we look around her home, standing first on one foot, and then on the other.

I offer our young friend a cigarette. The Spirit tells him his wife is very beautiful, a truth which he repeats to her in their own tongue; whereupon she breaks into a laugh and looks shyer than ever. We examine and admire her home, which I shall not describe, since it has much the same appearance as the Berber home we visited at Azrou: it is bare and primitive, without any of the comforts you would expect a young bride to possess. Several pitchers of water stand in one corner; the husband tells us there is no water in the *ksar*, it must be fetched from the river. We step out on to the flat roof. The family bedding is laid in the sun: a couple of rush mats and some bright rugs, hard couch for a bride. From here we can see over the flat house-tops of the village. Here and there women are idling or at work on their roofs, some grinding corn with primitive stone mills, others gossiping together. Our appearance at once causes a stir, and all work is stopped as the villagers stare across at the unexpected sight of two Europeans in their midst.

When we go down again, having increased the happiness of these two by expressing still more admiration for their home, I ask the young man if there is a living *marabout* in the village, and whether it is possible to see him.

Yes, says he, but he is now a very old man with few years to live; a very holy man who does not like now to be disturbed in his meditations. But if we wish, he will lead us to the old man and request an audience.

We set off again through the rabbit warren, and presently arrive at a doorway distinguished by being outlined in white. Our guide's knock is answered by a voice which has in it the querulous sound of old age. A brief conversation follows, then our friend leads us in. At the top of the stairs we come upon an aged man, very dirty, who sits cross-legged on a rug against the wall of his mud chamber. His eyes are dim and sunken, his face like bleached parchment above his white beard. He must be ninety years of age or more. He mumbles something unintelligible as his weary old eyes rest on us.

" He asks what it is you wish to know," says our friend.

" What *do* we want, anyway?" the Spirit asks me.

" I don't know. Better ask for his blessing, I suppose."

So our young Berber translates to the old man, who after a long silence raises a feeble hand and mumbles again. Then he gives a slow, weary roll of his head, and our friend says that he has finished, he is tired, and we must depart. The *marabout* is poor, he adds, and it would be a kindness if we could leave him a little money. Also he is blind, which is a great affliction for a man.

I drop a few francs at the old man's feet and we scramble down the narrow stairs, leaving the holy one staring before him with eyes that already seem lifeless. Soon he will be dead, and they will put his body in one of the little white-domed houses that men call *koubbas*; and those who are young men now will in their old age kneel before his corpse and pray, as we saw them praying out there in the *ksar*, and women will ask his bones to grant them the boon of children.

Our young friend, who tells us his name is Mohamma, walks with us through the *ksar* back to the entrance, where the elders still sit in the shade contemplating the peace of the palm grove and the distant hills, whose colour has darkened now to a deep mauve. One of the old men wears a mauve *djellab* and hood. He is a magnificent type of Berber, with fierce blue eyes and the expression of a puzzled, rather resentful animal. The Spirit is desperately anxious to paint him, and we ask Mohamma if such a thing would be possible.

"He is the brother of my father," he answers, "I will ask him."

Whereupon the two hold long converse together. At first the old man is truculent. He shakes his head, his speech is vigorous, and it is evident that he is refusing our request. But his nephew persists, and presently it seems that the old man is becoming tractable.

"I have told him that you have received the blessing of the *marabout*," says Mohamma at last. "He says that if the *marabout* will also bless the picture that you make of him, then it will be well."

"Can that be arranged?"

"I think it is possible. I will speak to the *marabout* and tell him that you are good people who will help him."

A little bribery, it seems, is all that is necessary to circumvent the decrees of Mahomet. But I warn the Spirit that she is preparing for herself grave complications in her After Life. It is said that when Mahomet was asked the reason for his objection to the arts, he replied that on the Judgement Day Allah would command the artists to give life to the figures they had made. This, he intimated, would put the artists in great distress, for who can give life but Allah himself?

"I'll take the risk," says the Spirit. "If the *marabout* puts matters right with Allah for a few francs, I don't see why I should worry. You see how useful it is to be friends with a saint."

So it is planned. We are to return to begin the picture in the morning, and meanwhile Mohamma will have whispered his words of temptation in the ear of the holy man. We shake hands with the old chief and his friendly nephew before we set off to the bungalow of M. Berujon.

After another of his excellent dinners we walk through the dark town to the café where we had promised to meet the young German Legionnaire. It is a dingy little place, but the only one that Ksar es Souk can offer. A few battered tables and uncomfortable chairs are set out under its arched colonnade of mud. Our Legionnaire is sitting there with three companions, all German, who rise and greet us with stiff little bows. They have a bottle of wine between them, and we join in the round that finishes it before we order another. Our friend of the morning is rather a serious young man, but his companions are more lively, and presently one of them produces a guitar and strums a German air while we talk and drink.

By degrees we learn a little of the past lives of these men. Our friend tells us that he was a clerk in Hamburg before he joined the Legion. He tired of the monotony of his life, and the urge for adventure was stimulated by seeing the ships leaving the port for the distant places of the world. So one day he too boarded a ship, taking with him the little money he had saved; and when that was spent on a jaunt through Italy and Tunis, he joined the Legion as the only alternative to returning to the hum-drum life. And now, says he, life is even more monotonous than it was back in Hamburg.

The man who plays the guitar was a student at Heidelberg until his father was killed in a Nazi putsch which deprived the son of income, so that his university education came to an end; and because of the bitterness he felt for the rulers of his own country he left to seek a living elsewhere, and so drifted into the Legion.

The third man is a seaman, the fourth gives no information about himself, so we may presume that his past is of a kind that merits secrecy. He is the toughest of the four, with a hard mouth and a wary eye, and he takes no part in the conversation.

Presently the guitarist strikes up a German student's song, relic of his days of prosperity, and two of his companions join in the singing; the fourth, the secretive fellow, remains mute, drinking steadily, smoking incessantly.

"He has the *cafard*," says our friend.

Now *le cafard* is the mental malady which at times afflicts all Legionnaires. It is a compound of black depression and sullen rage, fed by a monotonous life, by memories, by loneliness, by remorse and regrets and knowledge of opportunities wasted in the past. In the grip of *le cafard* a man is no longer responsible for his actions; he will quarrel, he will fight, he will desert, he will even take his life. This sullen fellow looks to us as though he is ready for any devilment. The more he drinks, the more sullen he grows. But he cannot damp the rising spirits of the others, who are now in full song. They insist that I too shall give them a song, and though I am no vocalist, with the Spirit's assistance I manage "Widdicombe Fair" with tolerable results.

So the evening passes pleasantly enough with these strangely assorted companions, and it is late when they escort us back to the hotel, where we have to rouse M. Berujon's negro guardian from his hard couch beside the front door before we can go to bed.

4

Mohamma and his uncle are waiting for us at the entrance to the *ksar* when we arrive at eight o'clock next morning. The old man is grim and fierce as ever, but he seems to be resigned to his fate. Mohamma tells us that all is well, the *marabout* has promised to give his blessing to the picture, so we can now proceed.

He is an excellent sitter, this old chief, for he has all that oriental placidity and resignation which makes the perfect model. For two hours or more he squats here at the entrance of his village, moving scarcely a muscle; modelling is no strain to him, so that he never needs a rest. He treats the business of being painted with a supreme indifference which is not, however, shared by the rest of the village. Soon the Spirit is the centre of a crowd of fifty or more people who hem her in on all sides. There is the inevitable crowd of half-naked brown Arab and Berber children, shy girls from the *ksar*, women carrying on their shoulders their great amphoras of water from the river, bearded

old men of solemn mien and courteous manners —
all must join the crowd to see this magical reproduction of the grim old chief.

When the picture is finished about noon the old
man takes his first look at it. He studies it for a while,
makes some comment which we do not understand,
and dismisses the matter. Mohamma, who is himself
delighted with it, tells us that his uncle approves, and
it will now be necessary to take it to the *marabout*. So
the four of us set off into the *ksar*, followed by the
crowd, which waits outside when we enter the holy
man's hovel and climb the narrow stairs. The old
chief has some talk with the *marabout*, then Mahomma
lays the still wet canvas at his feet. The blind man
raises his palsied hands and makes a few passes over
the picture which he cannot see; he mutters a few
sentences, and the trick is done. The picture is blessed
by the holy one. It is sanctified. It can bring no harm
to the old chief.

"How much for the blessing?" I ask Mahomma.

"Whatever you wish," he says.

"Ten francs?" I hazarded.

"Whatever you wish," he repeats.

So I give the old man his francs and we scramble
out of the presence.

"A very cheap blessing, I call it," says the Spirit,
who is so pleased with her morning's work that I think
she would have paid ten times the price if it had been
necessary. Before we leave the *ksar* I give ten francs
also to Mohamma for his trouble. He accepts it with
a quiet "*merci bien*," and we part with a mutual
promise to meet again before we leave Ksar es Souk.

A charming fellow, Mohamma. He belongs to the
race of southern Berbers whom the Arabs call the
Chleuh, the cast-out folk; but the Chleuhs call themselves the Amazcight, or noble people, since they
consider themselves superior to the Arabs who

overran their country and conquered all except the fastnesses of the Atlas mountains. And indeed there is a nobility in the bearing of these wild people which well justifies their name . . .

They were happy days that we spent among them, wandering through the palm groves or by the exuberant waters of the Ziz; bathing sometimes in its blue pools; or exploring the mysteries of the great *ksour* built every half mile or so along its banks. Each of these walled fortress villages is a self-governing community, very jealous of its independence, carefully guarding and tending the precious land around it from which comes the sparse living of the people.

One day while the Spirit sat painting on the blue and white shore two little boys approached and hung around at a distance. They seemed to be shy of approaching too near; so presently I produced two apples from our lunch bag and held them up invitingly. The boys came forward warily, as though they suspected some trick; they were like animals that are not sure of the intentions of their coaxer. When they were convinced that I had no evil designs they came up and took the fruit, sat down near us to watch the operation of painting, and talked to us. One was a hunchback with a dark skin and features that suggested a negro somewhere in his ancestry; but he had large lustrous brown eyes and a bright intelligent countenance with an expression of great gentleness, a characteristic that was shared by his companion.

When our friendship was well established they became very attentive. The hunchback was solicitous of the Spirit's comfort. He removed stones from the spot where she stood and helped her to shift her easel. His friend went off to gather some of the mauve and blue flowers that grew among the rocks, and presented them to us.

The boys spoke fluent French, and soon the talk

turned to work. What did they intend to do when they grew up? I asked, wondering what would be a Berber boy's equivalent to an English boy's passion for engine driving or aeroplane piloting. The hunchback's friend said he wanted to be a soldier with a gun; but the hunchback's ambition was to be a teller of stories.

Now this was interesting, and I encouraged the boy to tell us more of his ambition. I reminded him of Mahomet's belief that nothing is mightier than a fairy tale told by a wise man, and of how the Prophet would lean against the trunk of a palm tree and put his messages in the form of fairy tales. There was a great art, I told him, in the telling of tales, and the teller gained much honour and sometimes money, as I had seen in the cities of the north where he had never been.

With this encouragement he offered rather shyly to tell us a story, so the three of us sat in a semi-circle before him while he spun his romance in his own language. He spoke well, improving as he warmed to the tale, and used many gestures to illustrate his points. The story, his friend said, was about a wicked *djinn* with one eye, a terrible *djinn* that haunted the mountains and frightened the people, until one day it was destroyed by a young man of great courage and many arts. We did not gather exactly how the *djinn* was destroyed, but took it for granted that the method must have been effective. When he had finished I gave him a franc's worth of encouragement. He looked at the coin in his hand with a kind of wonderment in his bright eyes, then gazed up at me with unspoken gratitude: it was his first earning as a story teller. Perhaps in the days to come he may be seen in the market places of Meknes and Rabat holding the interest of the crowds with his talks, who knows . . . ?

*   *   *

Then there were pleasant afternoons spent in the garden of the Commandant, which runs beside the river. Roses climb over its blue pergolas, oleanders and geraniums of vivid hues grow exuberantly in the shade of its trees. And there were peaceful afternoons when we stayed in our rooms working to escape the heat of the sun. It was on such an afternoon that M. Berujon gave us one of his shocks.

He tapped on the door, burst in, and in that startling hoarse whisper of his said:

" *Pardon, monsieur, pardon, la maison est cassée.*"

We sprang to our feet, expecting the walls to come tumbling in on top of us. Behind M. Berujon stood two tall bearded Arabs in white.

" *Cassée?*" I exclaimed.

" *Oui, c'est cassée,*" he whispered, pointing excitedly into a far corner of the roof.

We stared up, but could see nothing except a small brown stain on the white muslin which was stretched across the beams that held the mud and wattle roof to serve as a ceiling.

M. Berujon explained. The house was broken, and he had brought the builders along to look at it.

It was a shameful thing, he said, that his new hotel should have a leak in the roof, just because there had recently been a shower of rain.

You must realise that rain seldom falls in these regions, otherwise these mud houses could not long survive. The roofs are drained primitively by a wooden channel which projects through a hole in the wall.

The two Arabs bowed their way in, inspected the devastation, were deeply and sorrowfully concerned, promised that it should be remedied and would never happen again, were at a loss to understand how it could have happened at all — but, really, what could you expect when rain inconsiderately fell? — and departed with many regrets for the disturbance.

It was with real regret that we parted from M. Berujon to continue our journey. He had made us happy in his pleasant bungalow. We loved the peace and friendliness of this town of the oasis, where the tempo of life is restrained and men have time to be lazy and dream in the sun. If ever I want to escape from life, I think I shall go and live with M. Berujon.

CHAPTER 8.

Tells of a Merry Journey — Wrestle with a Goat — Pursuit by a Camel — Saharan Jews at Home — a Bargain — Painting Rahel — Dinner with a Legionnaire — Locked in for the Night — the Last Bus to the Sahara.

I

The pale white light of dawn is beginning to throw the hills into black cardboard silhouettes when we leave M. Berujon to catch a bus at five a.m. for Erfoud. Already there is a stir of life in the town. Some of the roads through which we pass are littered with small bivouac tents in which Arab and Berber traders have spent the night; candles and charcoal braziers glowing at their entrances are the only illumination in the town. The air is cold before sunrise, so that we are glad to crowd into the bus with a dozen men of the Legion.

Except for a Berber girl with a weeping eye, they are our only fellow-travellers on this journey, and a merry crew they prove to be. Five of them are Frenchmen, four German, two Czech and one Russian. When the bus starts they produce bottles of wine and long French loaves and cheese, and insist that we shall share their breakfast. So we trundle away into the wilderness at dawn, sipping raw red wine and eating goats'-milk cheese.

The merriest of the party is a young corporal who is for ever laughing and joking. He makes a fine display of love-making to the Berber girl, offering her with hand to heart a paper flower which he takes from his cap; while she, laughing, hides her face and perpetually dabs at the eye that will not cease from weeping. There is a tumult of talk and laughter that deafens in the confined space of the bus.

The driver, too, is a lively and garrulous fellow. His trouble is that he cannot talk without incessant and elaborate gesturing, so that he seldom has two hands on the wheel at the same moment. Sometimes to illustrate a point in his talk he must gesture with both hands at once, while the bus continues its way unperturbed by this lack of attention.

I ask the merry corporal the inevitable question — whether there are any Englishmen in his company. There is one, he says, and mentions the man's name; and a very popular fellow he appears to be, since he receives an allowance of two hundred francs a week from his family in England. I gather that this lucky man is generous with his wealth, and provides many a satisfactory evening among the "earthquakes."

The corporal says he belongs to the mounted section of the Legion. Every two men have a mule between them. When they are campaigning they take turns in riding and walking, and so in a day's march can cover forty to fifty miles. He says he is taking his men to Erfoud, where they will collect their mounts before passing out into the *bled*, the country, for a few weeks' patrolling.

The sun has risen now, and the barren wilderness of rock through which we pass glows red-brown in the slanting rays, and the distant hills change from purple to rose. Presently in the distance the colour of the land changes to a bright yellow.

"It's the real desert at last," says the Spirit.

And so it seems. Soon we plunge along a track that runs through billows of sand, which rises in long surges to crests that glisten in the morning light and sinks in troughs where a man could hide in the shadow. It has exquisite curves and contours. Breezes play over its surface, drawing little wisps and eddies into the air, where the sunlight turns it into yellow spray. A mile or so further on the sand ends abruptly and we are back in the rocky wilderness, where there is no more genuine desert.

It is a disappointment, and I remark on this phenomenon to our corporal, who explains that the sand has been brought there from the desert by storms. Apparently some peculiar formation of the land and the hills creates a channel through which the air currents pass until they reach this region, where they are no longer able to carry the sand, so deposit it here, making a miniature desert in the wilderness.

The shattering truth about the Sahara, as we were later to learn, is that only about a tenth of it is sand. The remainder is like this barren rocky country through which we have been passing, with ranges of low hills and plains of brown stone. In the centre of the Sahara lies a range of mountains comparable with those of Switzerland, whose peaks carry snow through half the year. And oases are no mere puddles fringed by a few straggling palms, but fertile regions some-times hundreds of miles in extent. There is plenty of water in the desert, fifty or sixty feet down, as the sinkers of artesian wells have discovered.

Another illusion which we have lost concerns the temperature of the desert. By day, it is true, the heat is blistering; but the nights are frigid, and we shiver under the thickest of coats. When the sun has gone, and the cold wind blows strong across the wastes, we know that those torrid desert nights beloved of romantic novelists and film producers were born in the imagination . . .

Now we are again in the valley of the Ziz, where the palms grow beside the water, and yellow *ksour* raise their tall walls and towers. As we approach one of these villages there is a great to-do at the entrance. A tall lean old Berber is waving us to a standstill. Follows a palaver with the driver, after which the old man darts back into the *ksar* and presently returns struggling violently with a large goat. He wants to take it to Erfoud, but the goat has other inclinations. Evidently it would rather stay at home, and shows its preference by charging its owner, getting tangled up in his flowing *djellab* and bringing him to the ground.

Cheers from our Legion companions, who watch the struggle with enthusiasm while urging on the goat to further conquests.

At last the old man manages to grapple with the goat at close quarters. After a little in-fighting he lifts it bodily. Its forelegs are round his neck, its hind legs embrace his waist, while its head peers round the side of his turban. Thus the old man and his captive mount the step ladder to the roof of the bus where, if we are to judge by the thumping and bumping above our heads, the struggle is continued with unabated vigour. When the bus starts again we can watch the fight in shadow thrown on the desert by the sun. It seems for a while that the goat is winning again, until at last the old man gets an effective stranglehold on his opponent, so bringing this perilous all-in wrestling to an end. He spends the rest of the journey lying on the conquered animal to keep it quiet.

On the roof we now have four Berbers, one goat, half a dozen fowl, and numerous bags of grain in addition to other luggage. Luckily our own baggage is stowed in the back of the vehicle, otherwise it might not have fared well amid the wrestlers. All these diversions have given our driver a good deal to talk about with voice and hands, so that the bus enjoys frequent spells of liberty, wherein it behaves in its usual exemplary manner. I confess that at first I feel a little nervous of this erratic driving, but since nobody else seems to worry I gradually get back my confidence in the vehicle's good sense.

After sixty miles of this rough travelling, we rattle into Erfoud, chief town of the oasis of the Tafilalet, land famed for its dates and dust storms and merciless sunshine, cradle of the Alaouites, whose dynasty in the past ruled the whole of Morocco.

2

It is no later than nine a.m., we are parched for coffee, and we set off through the town in search of a café. The rough streets have much the same aspect as those of Ksar es Souk; they are wide between the low flat red boxes of houses, planned in definite lines like an American city; but they are improved by the introduction of pale green tamarinds. Outside every low doorway one of these trees flourishes, giving cool shade to the families who come out of their homes and squat during the heat of the day. They are a good-looking race of people here; dark skinned, half-negroid, many of them, but friendly and ready to go out of their way to help us.

We find two cafés in the main square of the town. They are barren, barrack-like places. One glories in the name of *Café Glacier*, the other of *Hôtel et Café de la Palmeraie*. We choose the second, because it sounds more imposing. A negro greets us in the bare room, where there is a counter made of pink cement into which coloured pebbles from the river bed have been pressed to make a pattern. He puts out a rickety table and chairs for us under the arched colonnade, receives our request for coffee, bread and butter with a very worried expression on his face, and proceeds to execute the order.

First he has to run out for milk. Then he must send a boy helter-skelter for butter. When these things arrive the coffee is tepid, the bread like rock, the butter rancid. We feed the bread and butter to a little hunchback boy who lurks half-naked round our table, murmuring pleadingly but with an engaging smile for something to eat. There seem to be a good many hunchback children in these parts. This child is a bit of a humourist; he smacks his lips, rolls his eyes, rubs his tummy, and grins when he has finished, a proceeding which is more eloquent to us than his unintelligible words. I suppose he seldom enjoys such a treat as rancid butter.

On one side of the square where we sit is the walled entrance of the Foreign Legion barracks and the local court of justice or administration, where groups of white-robed *sheikhs* and *caids* squat around in the shade awaiting the hearing of their claims. The other side is occupied by the low arched façade of the *souk*. Hither we wander when we have paid for our coffee.

We find all the usual commodities needed to keep life in the human body, but little else. There are grains and rock salt and chunks of meat black with flies, spices and herbs, dates packed in goatskin, but no silks or satins, nothing for the adornment of the body. There are signs of great poverty here, and the people are ragged, and shy like untamed animals.

The Spirit finds some native dishes made of woven rushes, roughly patterned with black, which intrigue her so much that she buys one. It costs her only a franc, which is proof of the poverty of these people: the dish, closely woven and three feet in circumference, must have cost some man or woman at least a day's labour, for which three halfpence seems poor pay.

When she finds herself among peasant-made goods there is no holding back the Spirit; she will buy up half a market unless I restrain her with a reminder that we have no pantechnicon with us.

It was while she was enjoying herself in the market that we saw the baby camel. It stood beside its lofty, contemptuous mother, looking like something out of a Christmas toy bazaar. It was a delicious creature, three feet in height, fluffy and ingenuous, with an expression of intense surprise on its face.

Of course the Spirit must needs go across to pet it; whereupon the parent camel betrays a most aggressive maternal instinct and an ill-temper which is the characteristic of all camels. She stares down haughtily for a moment, then with a grunt and a bubbling snarl and a swoop of her long neck she comes across at the Spirit with bared teeth.

The Spirit gives one startled glance at those yellow incisors, large as piano keys, before she flees, with the camel in long-legged pursuit, and its infant uttering bleating cries as it follows mother. Across the market the Spirit runs, dodging round the small piles of merchandise, which the camel, having no such scruples about other people's property, scatters with her hooves. There is a hubbub in the market and a running of many feet; and the pursuit is arrested only when its owner, a gaunt brown old Arab, charges up and fetches mother a whack across the snout with his staff, while he seizes her halter. Whereupon the camel utters a final snarl before turning her attentions to her offspring, who takes the opportunity to find consolation and nourishment in the manner of all babies.

The danger over, we join in the laughter that sweeps through the market. These people have a simple sense of fun, and they have appreciated this diversion. The cameleer explains at great length and in his own tongue the reason for his beast's hostility. We do not understand, but whatever the explanation may be, the Spirit has one of her own.

"I'm sure it's my hair again," she says. "If this sort of thing goes on I shall have to hide it under a turban."

I think that we in England have a good many illusions about the camel, fostered no doubt by happy childhood experiences at the Zoo. If you would know the truth about this oddly-conceived creature, I will tell you that he is invariably ill-tempered, stupid, stubborn and ungrateful. When he decides that work is not congenial, he can be more stubborn than a thousand mules. He is untamed and untameable. Neither the mangy brown creature that is the sole capital of the poor trader nor the magnificent cream-coloured *mehara*, the racing camel of the Tuareg, will ever be your friend.

But without him the desert dweller would be lost, for he provides his master with porterage, clothes, shelter, milk and often food. Camel's hump stewed is a great delicacy. The best camels can travel fifty miles in a day, and live four days without water. His wool is woven into tents, his dung is used for fires, and he lives to a ripe old age of forty-five or more. But if you want something on which to lavish your affection, pray do not pick upon a camel.

When we leave the market we walk through streets where the windowless houses are washed with pale rose colour and have doors of lemon yellow. At the doorways and under the tamarinds sit women and girls wearing magnificent costumes of a kind we have not seen before during our journey . . .

The most prominent feature is the headdress. It consists of an enormous roll of wool shaped like a saveloy, curved across the head from ear to ear, and covered with striped red silk. The head beneath is shaved. Enormous metal earrings, some of them ten or twelve inches in circumference, hang from the ears, and are so heavy that they have to be supported by a chain passing over the head. Their dresses are in vivid greens and reds, and they wear white aprons finely embroidered in red.

One of these girls throws us some laughing remarks as we pass, and this gives us an excuse to stop and investigate. I want to take her photograph. The girl is willing to pose, but asks first how much I will give her. I offer a franc. No, she says, that will not do; two francs. All right, two francs. No, three francs, she adds. Two francs, say I, making a gesture to put my camera away. All right, two francs, and the money in advance.

Now we are surprised at this bargaining spirit, for we have not encountered it since we left the northern cities on the other side of the Atlas. When the photograph is taken the Spirit asks the girl what her dress represents, what tribe, what race; and she tells us that it is the dress of the Saharan Jews.

" I've got to paint this girl," says the Spirit. " I've never seen such a magnificent costume."

When we broach the subject to this girl, whose name we learn later is Rahel, she runs back into the house, excitedly displaying her two francs, and a moment later brings out the whole family. Her father is an elderly bearded man in black gabardine and skull cap; her mother an ample Jewess wearing a costume similar to that of her daughter; there is a brother as well as several young sisters. The rest of the street's inhabitants, seeing the excitement, also emerge, and soon we are the centre of a crowd of some sixty people.

The father speaks only a little French, but it is enough to enable him to bargain. How much will we give to make a picture of his daughter?

" How much is she worth?" I ask the Spirit.

" Better start low," she says. " This looks as though it will be a tough job."

I begin by suggesting, firmly and decisively, five francs.

Rahel laughs her derision. Her father shakes his head, spreads his hands and explains that Rahel will be taken from her work, which is lace-making for the *souks* of Fez and Marrakech, and her work is well worth more than five francs, it is worth twenty-five francs for the afternoon.

After much argument we compromise at fifteen francs, about one and tenpence, and I think Rahel is well pleased with the bargain.

When we have brought our luggage from the bus office and engaged rooms at the Café Glacier, we return to the Jewish house, where I spend a lazy afternoon sitting on vivid red rugs on the floor with Rahel's family while the Spirit works outside. It is a pleasant house, consisting of a courtyard and several rooms with hard earth floors, whitewashed walls and practically no furniture. The father tells me he is a trader in cloths, and goes frequently to Marrakech, the metropolis of the south, in the course of his business. Once a year the whole family go with him for diversion. He is knowledgeable in the history of his race, and tells us that the Saharan Jews are descendants of the tribe of Naphtali. His ancestors came to Africa from Tarshish and Aleppo in the ships of the Phoenicians, who had colonies all round the coast of Morocco. They fled from the conquest of Shalmaneser the Assyrian. From the coast they spread through the Dra and the Sous and the Tafilalet to the borders of the Sahara and beyond, until now there are many thousands of the people of Naphtali in the land.

While we talk, Rahel is having the time of her life out in the street. She has been chosen above all others to be painted into a picture, she is the centre of local interest, and she is making the most of her brief glory before the envious eyes of her neighbours. But she is a restless model, and must constantly be running over to see how the picture is progressing. When it is finished she claps her hands excitedly and for a moment forgets to ask for her fifteen francs.

Then the painting must be displayed for the inspection of the whole street before we are allowed to take it away. And then we must be followed down the street out of the ghetto, which men call *mellah*, by a crowd of women and children clamouring for their photographs to be taken for the sum of two francs, one franc, fifty centimes, anything.

It was through the sentry at the gates of the Foreign Legion camp that we met Legionaire Smith. I call him Smith, because I know that he does not wish his real name to be known. The sentry told us that there were two Englishmen in the corps at Erfoud; one would shortly be returning from a working party outside the camp. If we waited ten or fifteen minutes we might see him.

We tried to pick out the Englishman as the company marched smartly across the square through the gate, but he might have been any one of the score of men. The sentry followed them in, and presently Legionaire Smith came out.

He was a good-looking, well-built fellow of about twenty-seven, with blue eyes and the quiet voice of a man of culture. He shook hands with us, looking a little shy. We asked him to come across to the café for a drink, but he had to decline on the grounds that he was not allowed out of barracks till six o'clock; though he was happy to accept our invitation to dinner that evening.

It was a rough and ready dinner that they prepared for us in the Café Glacier — sardines, tinned tomatoes, rissoles, tough mutton, lentils, cheese, dates and wine — but the best they can do in these parts. There is no green-stuff, since rain has not fallen at Erfoud for five years. But Legionnaire Smith enjoyed it well enough; and he enjoyed even more the chance of talking to English strangers.

There was one other Englishman with him,* he said, but after a year of association they couldn't find much to talk about between themselves. In the course of the evening we learned a good deal about Smith. He belonged to a county family in the Midlands. He had been a subaltern in a famous English regiment, which he had been obliged to quit because, as he explained, "the climate became a little unhealthy for him." He assured us, however, that it was for no criminal act. Well, it seemed there was nothing for it but that he should continue soldiering, so he joined the Legion. He had had four years of it, and would be free in a year's time. He confirmed all we had already learned about the hard and monotonous life, but added that for him the worst part of it was the complete lack of mental occupation. His mind had slipped back so badly that he now could not do the simplest calculation without working it out on paper. At first he had been one of the rebellious recruits and had landed himself more than once in detention. His parents used to send him money, but this led him into the inevitable trouble — drink — and so to detention, and he had asked his parents to stop the allowance. Luckily he had escaped Colomb Bechar, which is the

* There was an interesting sequel to this meeting after we returned to London. Some of the Spirit's pictures were exhibited at the British Empire Society of Arts at Imperial Galleries, South Kensington. In the resultant publicity, several newspapers told stories of her adventures in Morocco and mentioned Erfoud. A few days afterwards she received a letter from a woman at a North London address, who after apologising for writing, explained that she had read the reports of our visit to Erfoud and was anxious to know if we had met her husband, who was stationed there. We invited her to tea, and learned that this husband was Smith's companion. He was an English colonel's son, had landed in complications with some other woman, and gone off to join the Legion. It was some months before his wife knew what had happened to him. She was now taking divorce proceedings. But we could see that she was still in love with him. She was eager to know the kind of life he led, and whether the Legion was as terrible a place as she had heard. We were able to reassure her that it wasn't so bad.

penal settlement away in the Sahara, where very bad Legionnaires are sent. Here everything has to be done "at the double," and there are severe punishments. One of them, which seemed to us exceedingly silly though no doubt annoying to those on whom it is inflicted, is to make the men exercise by rolling over and over on their backs with their dinner held in their hands — after which, as Legionnaire Smith explained, there wasn't much left for dinner.

As for the food, he said, he did pretty well. At *réveille* each man has coffee, a slice of bread, and a morsel of sausage or salami. The main meal, served at ten-thirty a.m., and known as *soupe*, consists of broth, meat and vegetables, sometimes a pudding, half a loaf, a pint of wine and coffee. At five o'clock the midday meal is more or less repeated. His pay, after his four year's service, is seventy-five francs a half month, or about five shillings a week, which sounds little enough in terms of English money, but goes a long way in Morocco. We gather that he would be getting more if he had not been in trouble earlier in his career with the Legion.

And what, I asked him, did he intend to do when he left the Legion?

He shrugged.

"Something in the colonies, I expect," he said with a smile. "Isn't that the traditional thing for a black sheep to do?"

We were a little sorry for Legionnaire Smith, especially when we felt his lingering handshake at parting. We had talked a good deal about England and London, and I think he was disturbed by the memories we had revived. I tried to cheer him up by reminding him that he would be home in a year.

"A year's a long time here," he said wistfully. "Trouble is, one has to live it day by day, and every day is like the next. If only we could have a *war*."

When our guest has gone we have a talk with the young Frenchman who runs the Café Glacier. We compliment him on his dinner, which pleases him, and in particular we praise the icy coldness of his wine, asking whether he has a refrigerator. No, no, no, monsieur, he has no refrigerator, no ice, but he has a method which he is eager to show to us, and I can recommend it to you, for I have since tried it with good effect.

He wraps up every bottle of wine in six feet of flannel, winding it round until he has produced something that looks like a fat mummy. Then he soaks the mummies in water and keeps them in a dark cool place. Every hour or so he has water sprinkled over them, and so produces on request a deliciously cold wine in a hot country. Flannel, he points out, retains the cold as well as the heat, and we are not the first to have complimented him on his good wine.

We ask about our beds, which we have not yet inspected. He takes up a large bunch of keys and leads us out of the café. We walk about a hundred yards up the dark street and he unlocks a door in a blank wall, lights a candle, leads us through a chamber that might be a stable and up a flight of stairs made of pink mud mixed with chopped straw, which proves, says the Spirit, that the builders here have not suffered from the deprivations that caused the poor Israelites so much misery under Pharaoh.

We are going upstairs to bed. I hope you will appreciate that this is an unusual proceeding in a country where there is seldom an upstairs to go to. We emerge on a mud balcony over an open courtyard where a fig tree grows. We have two small iron bedsteads in a mud-walled, concrete-paved room. It costs 12 francs or one and sixpence the night. We have a window and an iron washstand with a pitcher of water beside it. A piece of mirror is somehow hitched to one of the walls by a cunning manipulation of slanting nails.

" *Petit déjeuner* in the morning?" asks our host.

" Please. Early."

" *Au revoir, monsieur et madame. Dormez bien*," he says, and is gone.

We do, in fact, sleep well — in sole possession of the hotel of Café Glacier, with the front door locked on the outside and nobody to disturb our dreams.

3

We discover next day that there is only one more bus on the Sahara route. It runs every second day to Rissani, some thirty miles further on into the desert. But when we reach Rissani, we are told, there is nowhere to stay, so we must return the same day.

Well, we make the journey. It is dusty and hot. The land is barren and with little interest. We have no adventures and no encounters worthy to be mentioned. We see the great *kasbah* of Rissani, meet a caravan of a dozen camels laden with merchandise on their way to the north, take a photograph or two, and return.

It was a journey wasted; we should have done better to stay in Erfoud and spend the time exploring the oasis. But at least it gave us the satisfaction of having reached the furthest point southward to which it is possible to travel by bus.

Now we must return to Ksar es Souk, where we can take a bus westward along the far side of the Grand Atlas, into the lands of the great Glaoui, Pasha of Marrakech and one of the three Lords of the South.

CHAPTER 9.

Tells of Lipstick in the Wilderness — the Jew of the Willing Heart — Butchers' Shops in Trees — Encounter with Emperor Jones — Power of the Caids — Alarm at Evening — Invitation from a Sheikh — Appeasing the Djinns — Donkey Ride with Ait Derduri and Son — A Party in a Mud Castle — Strange Wedding by Night — the Power of an Apple.

I

There are no roads now. The routes by which we travel are called by the French *pistes carrossables*, tracks which can be used for vehicles, but cannot be recommended for easy travelling. They pass through the same barren, yellow-brown wilderness of dust and stones which I have already described.

Sometimes we pass a *ksar*, sometimes the *kasbah* of a local caid, or a mud village deserted and crumbling to dust in the blaze of the sun. Once we plunge through the shallow waters of a river, get stranded on its opposite bank and have to alight to push the vehicle up the slope. Once we are held up for half an hour on the burning, silent plain by a breakdown, which the driver is happily able to remedy after much cursing in French and Arabic.

With the exception of a French girl, our companions are Arabs and Berbers. Now this girl is what the Spirit calls a dropper. She is perpetually losing things. First it is her gloves. Then it is her handkerchief. Finally she upsets the entire contents of her bag on the floor, and there is much scrabbling under seats and among legs to recover her possessions. Finally she stops the bus, gets out in the middle of the wilderness, and walks away into the empty solitudes as nonchalantly as though she were going for an afternoon's shopping.

We are puzzled as to why a well-dressed, carefully made-up girl should come all this way to go for a walk in an uninhabited wilderness, and we seek enlightenment from the driver. He tells us that she is the wife of an officer who is on bivouac with his company away in the hills. She comes to see him every week by bus, and is driven back at night by car.

At the next stop an elderly Arab who gets aboard finds a lipstick on the floor. He offers it to the Spirit, who disclaims ownership. So with a gesture of disgust he throws it out of the window.

After about three hours hard going we rest for ten minutes at Goulmina, a Berber village with its walled *souk* and the inevitable barn-like café for travellers. Here all the native women are dressed in dark blue, and many have their black hair bobbed, with a fringe low over the forehead, giving them a Chinese appearance. We lose most of our travelling companions and take aboard a new group that includes a lively Berber boy of about fourteen years and his father, a fine type with aquiline nose and glowing brown eyes, dressed in purest white. They are evidently people of importance among their own kind, proof of which is given by the action of a retainer who sees them off. Before his master boards the bus this servant bends forward and kisses his shoulder, a sign of fealty to his chief.

These two display an undisguised interest in us. They lean forward in their seats and watch our every gesture and movement. Sometimes they smile at us, giving the impression of two people watching kittens at play. When later on I produce some thirst-quenching apples from our bag, I offer them to the father and son, who each accept one with a grace and charm of manner that make our own manners seem crude and barbarous in comparison. Each produces a long knife from under his *burnous* to peel the fruit.

This gift of apples was later to have a sequel which made one more pleasant memory for us to take away from Morocco.

A few more hours of weary jolting in the heat, another plunge through a shallow river, and we climb a hill to Tinerhir, which is to be our resting place for another few days. The new village, with its military encampment, stands on a barren brown hill in a plain circled by mountains that are sometimes brown, at other times rose, occasionally a deep blue, according to the time of day and the angle of the sun. Beside this hill runs the stony bed of a shallow mountain stream, Oued Todra, its banks fringed with palm groves above which rise the towers and walls of great *ksour*.

Our bus deposits us at the inevitable red mud bungalow which is a little barren café-hotel, whence hurries a quick, bright, eager little man in European clothes. He is so eager and smiling and friendly that we feel at home even before we have entered the bare room which serves as bar and restaurant. There is a fine display of assorted bottles on shelves behind the rough bar, tiers of tinned fruits and vegetables, and a big corner cupboard stocked with more tins.

He is happy to hear that we are staying. He will have *déjeuner* ready for us in ten minutes. Meanwhile he takes us into a courtyard behind the bar and shows us rooms, two bare concrete-paved chambers each with a vast double iron bedstead and a window protected by wrought iron grilles. We take the rooms at fifteen francs the day each. And then we discover that there are no keys to the locks, nor any bolts. He seems surprised that we should require to lock our doors; nevertheless he is off like a busy terrier after a rat, hunting high and low for keys. He returns with an assortment of all sizes, most of them rusty through disuse. He tries them all in the doors, but none is effective. What are we to do, then?

"But it is not the custom here to lock doors, *monsieur* and *madame*, truly it is not. There are no dishonest people here, nobody will come and rob you."

A little uneasily the Spirit accepts his assurances, vowing, however, that she will put the washstand against her door when she goes to bed, since only a six-foot wall separates her door and the courtyard from the desert outside.

Back in the bar room we sit before a white cloth spread on the only table which the place possesses, while the willing little man fusses happily around serving lunch. He has the spirit of willing, eager service which pleases us; there is none of the take-it-or-leave-it attitude which you might well expect to find when you realise that this is the only restaurant and hotel in the place.

Not only did he serve an excellent lunch, but cooked it as well; *hors d'oeuvres* of sardines, tunnyfish and beetroot all from tins, a delicious ham omelette, *macaroni au gratin*, crisp rolls with real butter, a jar of Crosse and Blackwell's peach jam, red wine and coffee. While we were eating one course he cooked the next and had it prepared to serve when we were ready. In swift and efficient service he could set an example to many a civilised restaurant I could name.

We find ourselves unable to place his nationality. Although his French is fluent, there is something so free and ungrudging about him that suggests he is not a Moroccan Frenchman, and although he is brown-skinned, he is not an Arab nor a Berber.

I put the question to him.

"I am an Israelite of Marrakech," he said, drawing

himself up a little proudly and with just a hint of
defiance in his manner.

"Naphtali?" I suggest.

"Naphtali, *monsieur*."

"We have some good friends among the people
of Naphtali in Erfoud," I tell him, to ease the slight
tension I felt my question had caused.

You must know that the Jew is still despised and
disliked by the Arab in Morocco, even though under
French rule he is no longer persecuted. There was
the consciousness or the memory of this persecution
in the manner in which our little friend answered my
question.

After lunch he insists on taking us down to the
village. He produces a small negro boy to carry the
Spirit's painting apparatus. He is full of information
which interests us. Among other things, he tells us
that two years before there had been a Berber raid on
his bar, and that four people had been shot down at
the counter.

"Yet you say it is safe to sleep without locked
doors!" says the Spirit.

"Ah, but now, madame, that is all changed. There
are no more dissidents now. They have learned that
it pays to be peaceful."

Down in the open space beside the towering mud
walls of the *ksar*, with a fringe of oasis palms on one
side of us and the wilderness on the other, we wander
through the busy market. Except for one or two
details, it is like other Saharan markets. But its shops
are original.

Consider, first, the butcher. At one end of the
square stands a row of stunted dead trees, baked
white by the sun. On their branches the dealer in
meat hangs his goods. If you require a chunk of
stewing meat, or a hunk of fat for boiling, you
make your choice from the most likely-looking tree,

bargain with the butcher, and carry the goods away with you.

On either side of the square are rows of queer-looking structures like large beehives, their domed roofs built of light grey mud. These too are shops. Inside each of them sits a trader with his wares spread out before him on the floor. He must be a prosperous trader to afford one of these places; our friend tells us that the rent, payable to the *caid*, is at least five francs a day, or about sevenpence halfpenny.

And now we come upon one of the queerest cafés we have yet seen. It is built of mud piled up against the wall. It has no particular shape, but is about twelve feet long, with an irregular opening for a door and an uneven round hole for a window. Outside the hole that serves as a doorway, pots of delicacies are stewing on charcoal braziers. The place reminds us of some gnome's house in an Arthur Rackham illustration for a fairy tale. So quaint is it that the Spirit must sit down there and then to make a sketch.

At once we are the centre of a motley crowd of African types. Then from the doorway of this gnome's hut projects a gaunt black head, which inspects us for a moment before its body emerges as that of an enormous negro in a dirty white robe. With a vast grin of delight the man shambles towards us, talking excitedly, and insists on taking our hands and pumping them vigorously while he thanks us in unintelligible language for the honour. Thereafter he stands in the doorway, posing as Emperor Jones might have posed, ignoring possible customers till the sketch is finished.

Our Jew with the Willing Heart now introduces us to a lean brown native whom he described as the *mohtasib*, or market overseer. He is appointed by the local *caid*, or governor. He regulates prices, settles disputes, and acts generally as a peacemaker. This *mohtasib* gives us a few smiling words of greeting, wishes us happiness in Tinerhir, and continues his rounds . . .

Now the *caid* is a powerful man in these regions. His job is much coveted, for he usually becomes a rich man. He must, in fact, have a good deal of money before he can become a *caid*, because a caidship very often goes to the highest bidder. He is appointed by the Grand Vizier of the Sultan, who also becomes a very rich man in a very short time. Now if it costs the *caid* a good deal of money to get his job, he naturally wants a return, and the only way to achieve this is to squeeze the natives. I have heard that the greed of the *caids* has been curbed to a large extent by the French, but still they have many opportunities to dun the poor, which must always be the case in a country where corruption has for so long been the key-note of government.

The *caid* surrounds himself with his own people, who support him in the administration of justice. In every village he appoints a *sheikh*, who is responsible for the good behaviour of the people. Sometimes the *sheikh* is a relative, because nepotism is always a source of power. Hence you will see how easy it is for a man once in the saddle to retain his position, supported by members of his own family . . .

The *caid* of Tinerhir, whom they tell me is a just and honourable man, lives in a pale pink *kasbah* on the hill, whither we go when we have done with the market. Unhappily he is absent on business, or we could have met him; but we are permitted to enter his walled castle and wander through its outer chambers. A few horses and cows are tethered in the court, and some ragged old men who look like beggars sit at his door. The place has the aspect of a mediaeval castle. From its walls we can see for miles across this great cup among the mountains, with its numerous fortress villages among the winding palm groves that mark the course of the river. Over all these villages this *caid* rules, and in each village is his lieutenant. He is a little emperor in his own kingdom; and his kingdom can be shattered by a stroke of the pen of the Grand Vizier.

2

There are diversions at dinner this evening. The first occurs during the artichoke course. We do not like artichokes, so during the temporary absence of the Willing Heart, whom we do not wish to offend by rejecting the food which he so eagerly set before us, we pulled off the leaves and pretended we had enjoyed them. When he returned, his keen but friendly eyes observed that the succulent ends had not been chewed, so he assumed that we did not understand artichokes, gave us a demonstration on how they should be eaten, and waited while we went through the pretence of enjoying them.

While we are thus suffering there is a sudden bugle call from the crown of the hill where the camp lies. It is an unfamiliar call to us, but to the Willing Heart it seems to have a special significance, for he hurries from the bar and scans the distance. Other people, we notice, also seem to be excited. We go to the door, and see men streaming up the hill from the plain. They are running. Among them are native troops as well as Legionnaires. The Willing Heart tells us it is the alarm call, and runs across the open space in front of his hotel to ascertain the cause. When he returns he tells us that there is nothing to fear, there is some trouble among the tribes away in the hills, and the authorities have called in the troops as a precaution. But it is nothing. These tribesmen will often have quarrels among themselves, and the military like to be ready in case of need.

" Are you *sure* we don't need keys for our doors ?" asks the Spirit, watching the men doubling up the hill like streams of ants.

" Absolutely, *madame*. There is no danger, it is just a private quarrel somewhere."

The second diversion came after the *pièce de résistance*. We had chewed valiantly at the tough meat of the south, which was called mutton, but had the consistency of underdone leather strengthened with interwoven grey cords, when to the open doorway came two figures in white whom we recognised as the father and son companions of the bus.

They enter and greet us with a salute and smiles, and stand before our table while the boy, who unlike the father speaks French, apologises for disturbing us at meat. We thought at first that they had called in for refreshment but realise now that they have come to see us.

Then the boy makes a charming little speech, rather elaborate and evidently carefully rehearsed, in which he expresses their pleasure at our presence, explains that they had made enquiries and discovered that we were staying here, and would be honoured if we would be their guests the next day, after we have rested the night.

We reply that we shall be happy, we consider it an honour. The boy says that his father's house lies about five kilometres away, which is a long way to walk, so that they will call for us with mounts if we will indicate the hour it pleases us to be ready.

Any hour that is convenient to them, we intimate ; and so it is suggested and agreed that we shall be ready at five o'clock the next afternoon. Now the good-looking father joins in the talk. He speaks for perhaps half a minute in his dialect, we do not understand a word, but from the expression in his face we know he is paying us gracious compliments.

Finally we shake hands, each raises his hand to his lips, and they are gone.

Meanwhile, the Willing Heart, who has entered during this conversation and greeted our visitors, tells us that the father is a certain under-*caid* or *sheikh*, named Ait Derduri, who is head man of one of the villages down by the oasis, a man much respected in the district. He assures us that this Derduri is a good fellow and that we shall come to no harm in visiting him, for he is very hospitable.

While he talks he busies himself lighting an acetylene lamp, the only illuminant his hotel offers, and presently the drab room is filled with its white glare. One or two soldiers come in for a drink and soon depart. It is yet some days from the fortnightly pay day, says the Jew, so there is not much custom. This revives thoughts of the Foreign Legion, and we ask if there are any Englishmen stationed here. He thinks there is one, and when I express an inclination to buy this lone countryman of mine a drink, the Willing Heart offers to find the man, and sends his negro boy chasing out into the night to the barracks.

Five minutes later he returns — not with an Englishman, but with a young Dutchman and a German. The German is small, very blonde and excessively dull. His companion, the Dutchman, explains in halting English that the Englishman is in detention, so they have come in his place.

Over a round of "earthquakes" this man told us what purported to be his life story. He had inherited from his father, he said, a small stationery business in Holland, it had gone bankrupt, so he had collected what little money there was left, visited Paris, failed to get on his feet there, and so had joined the Legion. His wife, who he adored, had promised to wait for him.

The Spirit said later that she doubted whether he

was worth waiting for. I am afraid we did not believe his story. The man was pleasant enough, but one detected a shiftiness about him, and perceived that he watched us carefully to see if we accepted his story. No, our Dutch friend has done something a little more discreditable than go bankrupt.

When they have gone we stroll down the hill in the moonlight with the Willing Heart. There are dim lights in a few little tents scattered about the market-place, where wandering traders are settling down for the night. In the donkey park a few animals lie stretched on the ground in rest. At nine-thirty Tinerhir is going to bed.

Not far from the high walls of the *ksar* the little domed *koubba* of the local departed saint shines palely in the night against a background of palms.

As we pass a dim figure of some Berber approaches the tomb, knocks three times on the wall, deposits some object beside it, and after squatting down begins to talk in a loud voice.

Our Jew says the man is asking some boon of the saint. His knocking is intended to wake up the dead man's soul. The object he placed before the tomb is a dish of food. Often, he says, these people place offerings there in the hope of pleasing their saints. Also they will place it outside their own doors or take it to lonely places in the hills to appease *djinns* and prevent them from troubling. The hills around us are full of *djinns*, according to the Berbers.

"What happens to the food?" asks the Spirit. "Do the *djinns* take it?"

The little Jew smiled.

"It is eaten, though I would not say by the *djinns*. Some beggar, perhaps, who has no reverence for tradition. Or there are Jackals."

3

The Willing Heart is magnificent. He produces a bath for us in the morning, a splendid tin tub which he brings into the room with every sign of pride in his possession. And then the bath water comes along, brought from a well at the bottom of the hill in great pitchers on the shoulders of two women.

One of them is a gigantic laughing negress who wears a red handkerchief over her head. She too takes a pride in this bath, and inspects the water with profound care to see that it does not contain anything which has no right to be there. She is such a character that the Spirit sees in her a new model; and after we have had coffee a sitting is arranged, with much full-throated, gurgling laughter as Umaima, which is our negress's name, is induced to display her black charms beside a branch of red hibiscus.

The heat is so great to-day that we spend the afternoon in *siesta*, resting before our trip to the home of Derduri. We are looking forward keenly to this experience, for we have as yet had only a superficial glimpse of private life in a mud village.

Ait Derduri and his son came riding up the hill long before the appointed hour, for time is of little consequence in these regions, where clocks are unknown and dawn and sunset are the only divisions of day and night.

They are mounted on incredibly small donkeys, and behind them an older man, evidently a servant, rides a third donkey while leading a fourth. They dismount at the door of the inn, and after the usual greetings and kissing of hands we prepare to mount the two spare steeds.

Now we are no strangers to mule or donkey riding; it is a mode of travelling in which we have found much pleasure in the past. Some of our happiest wanderings were spent on mule-back in Spanish mountains. Hence we are renewing an old and pleasant experience when we go trotting down the hill on these sturdy grey mounts whose spindly legs look scarcely strong enough to support their own bodies, with Derduri and his son on either side of us.

The boy's name is Mahru, though in the spelling of it I may be wrong; Mahru cannot spell in French, and I must rely on phonetics. It sounds as though it should be spelt Mahru. He is a bright, happy lad, full of laughter and fun, and he chatters away as we ford the shallow river and amble through the palm groves. The things we tell him he translates to his father, who answers through the son, while his brown eyes glow at us with what the Spirit later describes as a positive fire of friendship.

We come at last to a *ksar* by the river, where old men, as always, sit at the arched entrance in the high wall. They greet Derduri and his guests with salutes as we pass through. We dismount here and walk through the dark places of the *ksar* until we come to an open space where stands Derduri's house. From the outside it looks like all other mud houses, except that it is larger. The lower part or entrance is not inhabited, but upstairs there are several fine rooms, their walls white-washed and decorated with coloured rugs, several of which also lie on the floor. As usual we express our enthusiasm for this fine house, and after Mahru has translated to Derduri and Derduri has thanked us in glowing terms for our appreciation, we climb higher to the flat roof, where we sit on mats while Derduri brews mint tea.

We stay here for a long time, sometimes talking, at other times dreaming and at peace, until the declining sun has set the clouds aflame and turned the distant rose hills to purple; then Derduri invites us with infinite grace to go down to eat.

We remove our shoes and sit on the rugs while the low table is placed in our circle, and Derduri's wife places before us the first course. She is a dark, smiling woman of about thirty-five, and she wears a coloured *caftan* with a row of silver medallions across her brow. She does not eat with us, for it is not the custom, but retires to the kitchen when she has served.

First we have wooden bowls of a kind of maize soup, which is strong flavoured but good. Then follows a *couscous*, a stew full of scraps of tender mutton, egg plants, some green vegetable which Mahru tells us are date palm shoots, the whole mixed with stewed pears and surmounted by dates. It is a delicious and appetising dish. Now comes a kind of pancake, which we take off the communal platter and dip in a bowl of honey before eating. After we have washed our hands we are given mint tea again.

It takes a long time to eat, this meal, and towards the end of it we have become aware of a hubbub out in the *ksar*. There is a beating of distant tom-toms, the shrill wail of a flute, and a sound of singing. Mahru tells us they are celebrating a wedding in the village.

Now this is something we cannot miss, and I ask if it is possible to see the affair. A few minutes later we are out of the house on our way to the wedding.

The din grows louder as we pass through the covered ways, our hosts holding rushlights to show the way. We reach an open space where there is a concourse of people outside a house. Most of the crowd hold candles and rushlights, and by their glow we can see a feast spread out on the ground: bowls of steaming food, bright coloured sweets, rich and puffy doughnut rings. Evidently there has been a tremendous effort to prepare a fitting accompaniment to the wedding, for these people are poor. The beaters of tom-toms stand round the door. There is a great talking and singing and laughter among the women, and sometimes they break into a strange chorus of high-pitched sound which is their method of showing applause and appreciation. I can describe it best by telling how it is produced. First form your lips into a small o, slightly bunched up, as though you were on the point of saying "when". Hold that, and make a co-ing sound, like a child imitating the whistle of a railway engine; and at the same time rapidly move your tongue to and fro across the inside of your lips. Imagine a score or more people making this sound simultaneously, and you will know what Moroccan applause sounds like.

We are asked to join in the feast, for these people are Derduri's friends; but we have already overeaten, so make only a pretence at tackling a dough ring. Presently another group surges through the village, hustling a young girl in their midst. Mahru says she is the bride, and they are bringing her to the husband's home. She is making a fine show of reluctance, and she is well covered so that we cannot see her face. Her advent is heralded by a renewed outbreak of that strange applause before she is ushered into the house and the door closed on her. The tom-toms beat and a wild shrill song is chanted.

I ask Mahru what happens next. He says they are waiting "until it is accompliahsed." I do not understand at first, but after further explanation it is borne in on me that we are waiting for the marriage to be consummated. The girl has been escorted to the bridal chamber and given to her husband.

"No wonder the poor girl seems a little embarrassed," says the Spirit.

The feasting goes on, and one senses that the excitement is growing. With our hosts we sit on the ground drinking tea, while Derduri talks with friends, and Mahru laughs and jokes with everybody. It must have been half an hour later when the door opens and a woman cries out something to the crowd of guests. Whereupon with a loud shout a wildly excited fellow produces an ancient pearl-inlaid Moroccan gun and fires a blank shot into the air, sign that the consummation has been satisfactorily achieved. (Although natives under the French Protectorate must not carry guns, I was told later that this rule is often relaxed for wedding ceremonies.)

This shot is the signal for a renewed outbreak of applause and drum beating. It is still going on when we returned to Derduri's house to take our departure. The pair ride back with us in moonlight that made the night almost as bright as day. Their servitor waits at the inn to take back the donkeys, which we learn later have been borrowed for the occasion. At the door the Willing Heart is waiting for us. And here, with many elaborate courtesies and expressions of goodwill, we part from Ait Derduri and his happy Mahru, after arranging to meet again so that Derduri can sit for his portrait. We watch them canter away in the moonlight.

Just before she went to sleep that night, the Spirit murmured, "All this wonderful evening — just because of a gift of apples."

Truly the power of an apple can be great in these sunny lands.

CHAPTER 10.

*Tells of a Rough Journey — Breakdown — Snowed Up —
Murder in the Legion — a Ride of Terror — Paradise of
the South — the Sultan of the Atlas — Dinner with a
Feudal Ruler — Meeting Place of the Dead — the Berber
who Worked for Bertram Mills — Afternoon in a Harem
— the Ways of a Slave Dealer.*

I

The thrice-weekly bus which was to take
us the two hundred and fifty miles from Tinerhir
to Marrakech was a little late, by our ways of
reckoning. It should have arrived about eight
o'clock one evening. It appeared at seven a.m. next
day.

It was a strange, battered object, loaded on top to
a height as great as its own with hay and legs of mutton
and ham, with cases containing bottles and an infinite
variety of odds and ends. It creaked ominously as it
swayed to a standstill in front of the inn. Its driver,
a tired-eyed Frenchman, who seemed to be exhausted,
slumped into a chair in the bar and asked for coffee.
His conductor, a dwarfish, ragged negro of gorilla-like
aspect, seemed as fresh as though he had just emerged
from slumber. The driver explained wearily to the
Willing Heart that there had been a little trouble with
the bus, they had been held up for a while. They had,
in fact, slept in the bus.

This unfortunate fellow left Marrakech in the
dawn the previous morning, travelled all day over
the most perilous roads in the country to reach
Tinerhir by evening; he had snatched a few hours
sleep in the vehicle during the night, and now after
an hour's rest proposed to return, reaching Marrakech

at eight o'clock in the evening. Truly a hard life for a bus driver.

Our passengers are Arabs and Berbers. While we are preparing to start, a lean, mournful Jew in the usual black gabardine gown and skull cap comes to one after the other of us, pleading that we shall pay his fare to Marrakech. He tells a long and pitiful story about a dying wife whom he must see. Everybody spurns him, several laugh at him. It seems that this is his regular tale when he wants a free ride. Eventually he pays his fare and sits miserably in the back, or second-class section of the bus.

After about two hours travelling through barren yellow lands and low hills we have the first break-down. The rickety bus is piled high again with merchandise, and carries a heavy load of passengers. While we alight and stand about in the sweltering plain for twenty minutes the driver and his Gorilla tinker with the engine. At last they locate the trouble in a choked petrol feed.

Another few miles, and the bus stops again. The driver plays about with the engine for a while, finds nothing wrong, looks at the petrol tank as an afterthought, curses, and proceeds to fill.

Now this entails an elaborate ritual. The petrol is kept in a receptacle like a dustbin on the roof among the luggage. The Gorilla scrambles up, removes the stopper of the bin, and lowers into the petrol one end of a length of rubber tubing, passing the other end down to the driver, who puts it to his mouth and sucks until petrol comes, thus creating a syphon. The fact that he has to spit out a mouthful of petrol is merely incidental. He allows the spirit to pour into the tank till it is full, then removes the tubing, which the Gorilla hauls back, scattering a shower of petrol on the floor of the bus, over which the driver lights a cigarette with complete nonchalance.

Off again, with the Gorilla sitting on the roof, dangling his legs over the side as he croons to himself some song about God-knows-what. Six times during the hundred and twenty miles to Ouarzazate, our first big stop, this bus broke down. The thing was falling to pieces. The bonnet was tied on with string. Parts of the engine were held together with wire. A few hundred yards from Ouarzazate a rear wheel buckled, and we had to walk the rest of the way.

When the bus was brought limping into the dusty town, the driver said we should have time for lunch, because it would be necessary to *faire les reparations*. I suggested that it would be a better plan to *faire un autre autobus*. He agreed, but asked what could he do? It wasn't his *cochon d'un autobus*. We left him with his Gorilla, ruefully examining the dilapidated vehicle, while we walked through the main street in search of food.

Ouarzazate, the new Ouarzazate, is a dull and ugly military camp of red bungalows, headquarters of the army command over the south and the valley of the Dades; but the country around is ruggedly beautiful, rich in palm groves and great *kasbahs*, well watered where the river Dades runs through its scorched lands from the Atlas mountains. In the hot and dusty main street we found a small hotel-restaurant presided over by the ubiquitous ample blonde of uncertain age, who took us into a *salle à manger* gaudy with table cloths in red, yellow and blue check. We went through the inevitable lunch of omelette, tough meat, sweet and cheese, served by a Berber girl of sullen mien, while our tired senses were numbed by an incessant clatter from the tongues of four of the loudest-voiced army officers I had ever encountered. These voices were so deep and loud and penetrating in the small low room that they killed all power of thought or con-centration. We were glad to get out of the place and go back to the bus, which was to start almost immediately.

We sat in the decrepit vehicle in the burning heat for two hours. The driver and the Gorilla came up from time to time to tinker with it or to argue. Once the Gorilla had a suck at the rubber tubing and filled up the tank : I think he liked the taste of petrol. Then for a long time the pair of them were absent. When I went to inquire at what time the bus really intended to start, I found the driver sitting despondently in the office.

"To-morrow morning at five o'clock," he said.

"We have to stay here the night?"

"There is no other way. To start now would bring us into the pass at night. I cannot do it."

The unfortunate fellow looked so worn out we could only sympathise with him and make the best of the situation. We went back to the bungalow, where the ample blonde received us with a great laugh and open arms.

"It is often so," she said. "But I have some good rooms."

At the back of the restaurant was a corridor open to the sky and planted with beds of hollyhocks. Six rooms on one side of this corridor constituted the hotel. At the far end, in a small dusty garden, was the hole in the floor called *toilette*. In its door had been cut a diamond-shaped aperture nearly a foot in length; so that not only could inmates gaze out upon the garden, but prospective visitors could look in to ascertain whether the place was occupied.

We walked out of Ouarzazate to the *kasbah*, where the Spirit made some sketches; but we had no adventures or encounters, so at sunset returned to the hotel and sat on the verandah till dinner time.

There was a good deal of talk in the restaurant about the doings of two men of the Foreign Legion, who appeared to have created a new nine-days wonder in the town. We heard that they had only that morning killed one of their comrades, robbed him, and deserted. Even while we were dining the military were hunting the countryside for them. Although we made inquiries we could not ascertain whether any of the men involved were English.*

In the morning we were called in the dark at four a.m., and after drearily forcing down some indifferent coffee and sour bread by candle-light in the bar, walked up to the bus. It was piled higher than ever with merchandise. The Gorilla, after protesting in vain to an adamant Frenchwoman that he could not find room for her trunk, was scrambling among bundles of hay and sacks of oats on the roof, trying to wedge in the unwanted baggage. The driver was rousing three Arab passengers and the mournful Jew who had made their beds on the seats of the vehicle.

But at last we were off — ourselves, two elderly Frenchwomen, four natives and the Jew — on a nine-hour run to Marrakech.

This is no journey for weak hearts. Nor is it one for a dilapidated vehicle like this bus of ours. We soon begin to climb steeply up the lower slopes of the western end of the Grand Atlas. We leave the yellow and brown lands, and twist and turn among pale grey mountains, through verdant gorges and along the sides of cliffs. After three hours of this we pass a

* In October, when we were back in London, we read the following in an English daily paper : "Paris — Two members of the Foreign Legion have been sentenced to penal servitude for life by military court at Casablanca, Morocco. The two men, Jean Felten and another who went by the name of Michael Strogoff, belonged to the first cavalry regiment of the Legion, and were stationed at Ouarzazate. They deserted last May after murdering a soldier named Freyes, who was in charge of the ammunition department. They stole some arms and escaped. Five days later they were arrested near a canteen at Ighem. They had just taken possession of a lorry, threatening to kill the driver if he did not hand it over."

mile-long column of mounted troops on the move, with artillery and tanks. They have to halt at the precipice edge to allow us to pass; one plunge of a restless horse would send man and mount hurtling a thousand feet to perdition. The elderly French-women have friends in the regiment, for they hail the commandant and other officers as we crawl past. The road becomes more tortuous, and the overloaded, top-heavy bus creaks and sways sickeningly as it skirls round hairpin bends. Distant snow-peaks begin to raise their heads amid the chaos of mountains.

Presently the reason for our cargo of hay and oats and bottles is explained. We emerge into a pass where tents are being erected beside a stream, so that the troops can camp. While the driver and his Gorilla help a few troopers to unload the cargo, we wander awhile, revived by the soft clear breeze in the sunshine after the fumy air of the bus. We are attracted by some white objects lying beside the stream and, investigating, find the bleached skeletons of a horse and man, picked clean by vultures. They tell of some Berber blood feud; it seems that man and mount have been shot down while they paused at the stream for water.

Relieved of the worst of its burden, the bus feels safer now, and the driver doubles his speed, so that we take the hairpin bends at thirty miles an hour. After half an hour the cracked windscreen is suddenly spattered with white, the sun is blotted out, and we are in the midst of a dense snowstorm. The driver pulls up and settles down to await its passing; he dare not move blindly on these perilous ways. For an eternity we sit there, unable to see more than a few yards around us, shut off from the world in this swirl of whiteness. We may, says the driver gloomily, have to stay all day and night, unless it passes; he has known such things happen.

After two hours the storm ceases abruptly, and we are rattling on in a cold sunshine.

And now begins the real heart-quaking part of the journey, the nerve-tasting, breath-catching, stomach-turning plunge into an insanity of mountains. They are like some stupendous picture conceived by a disordered mind. They are too vastly elaborate to be true, too fantastically coloured to exist outside imagination. Some times they are a bright red, sometimes silvery grey and yellow; or they leap from terra-cotta to green, then sombrely to mauve and black. Our bus curls its way round some peak five thousand feet up, and we see the unending vista of these coloured mountains stretching away, it seems, to the limits of the universe. We plunge down some long ledge on the façade of a precipice, and see the coloured peaks far above; then up again, and we glimpse far below the white road twisting and turning like a worm in pain for five miles through a great chasm two thousand feet deep.

We are mounting the rose-coloured side of a gorge a thousand feet deep by a series of shelves cut zig-zag on its face. Two feet of road separate us from oblivion. We are on the edge of nothing, somewhere near the sun; we are in the depths on the way to hell. Now we are crossing a narrow embankment built to a height of six hundred feet across a mile-wide canyon, or racing along a path that ends in space — but turns at a right-angle to slide for a straight mile into the uttermost depths. Once, on the edge of nowhere, we have to negotiate a fall of rock which leaves us only a foot of road-space to spare; and again we have to crawl like a wary animal past a gap where the road has fallen away into a chasm. It is stupendous, this road; magnificent, terrifying.

Our hands involuntarily grip the seats and our bodies are tense, as when one sits in a dentist's chair waiting for the pain; our breathing is caught and held, our stomachs fall away and leave a horrible emptiness, as when a giant racer at some exhibition park makes its dive into space. One of the Moors behind me groans suddenly and loudly, commending his soul to Allah, as we approach the edge of a precipice, then skirt perilously to the right and run along its edge. Steam hisses in clouds from the radiator, an inferno of heat and choking fumes from the overtaxed engine fill the bus.

Presently on a rare stretch of level road one of the elderly Frenchwomen, who has been turning her head away and hiding her eyes from the chasms, gives a feeble cry, " *Monsieur, arrêtez, arrêtez, Mon Dieu, arrêtez.*"

The accustomed driver gives her a glance, shrugs his eyebrows and draws up. The woman scrabbles blindly at the door, and when I have opened it she staggers out and collapses beside the road, violently vomiting. Her stomach has gone, her nerve has failed her.

She has five minutes rest and attention, and we are off again.

But the worst is over. We have rounded three hundred hairpin bends and survived them. We have spent four hours in these fantastic mountains and emerged unscratched. We have negotiated the greatest pass in the Atlas, governed, like all these mountains by the Glaoui of Marrakech, whom men call the second Sultan.

The slope becomes gentler, and presently we are among the foothills which are mere molehills rising to five hundred feet. Then we are back to the red earth of the burning plain, and the great rose-coloured tower of the Koutoubia Mosque of Marrakech, landmark for centuries to the men who have come from the Sahara and Timbuktu to trade and to fight, rises like a sentinel among the palm-groves that circle an Imperial City.

And if you think that I have exaggerated this ride over the Glaoui's pass, test me by trying it for yourself in a native bus.

If you are jaded and desire thrills, you will find them here.

But if you are weak in the heart and nerves, keep away. It might cost your life.

2

How can I begin to describe this oasis city of the desert which men called El Hamra the Red? Shall I tell of its loveliness beneath the azure sky, of its gardens and flat-roofed houses and palaces the colour of faded roses, rising behind vast walls among a hundred thousand palm trees, over which the distant snow cones of Atlas brood like white nuns holding aloof from a world of warmth and colour and passionate life? Or of its savage history since its founder Youssef ben Tachfin, father of the great Almoravide dynasty, decided to create for his glory a city among the southern people he had subdued in the days when William the Norman was yet only meditating the conquest of Britain? Or shall I tell of the ways of the people it shelters, and of those who come many days' journey from the far places of the mysterious south to taste the strange delights of this Mecca of trade and pleasure?

Battles have raged round these walls which for nearly a thousand years have protected its swarming crowds of Moors and Berbers, Jews and black men from the slaughtering hordes of desert conquerors. Dynasties have risen and died amid its palm forest, which grew they say from the date stones spat out by an invading multitude that encamped for months around its walls. The armies that conquered Spain and almost overran all Europe gathered here for their march across the country to the Mediterranean. Hither came Moulay Ismail the sadist of Meknes, destroying some of the city's loveliest palaces for no other reason than that he did not want them to rival those he was building in Meknes. History and romance and tragedy are built into the very walls of Marrakech . . .

We approach the ancient city through the new French town of Gueliz which has grown outside the walls; and at once we are surrounded by a beauty that no other town in Morocco can claim. Wide streets of white and pale rose houses are shaded from the fierce sun by trees that offer flowery cascades of mauve and blue beneath a sapphire sky. Bougainvillaea flaunts its purple glory from rooftops and walls, hibiscus adds its passionate fire, and the great bell-like lily-tree, *dhatura*, gives its white purity to the sun amid the orange and citron and banana; while climbing geraniums of vivid colouring make hedges for the gardens. There is an exuberance of brilliant growth in this new town, as though it had striven to capture the romance and fire of the old and express it in colour. It is an earthly paradise after the parched and barren lands that have held us for so many weeks.

We are a little tired of hard beds and dust-storms, tough meat and the general discomforts of the South; and when we have tipped our farewell to the bus driver and the Gorilla, we bundle our kit into a barouche and give the driver the magic word "Mamounia." Now the Mamounia was once the home of Mamoun, son of a great Sultan of the past. When he died it became a residence for ambassadors from Europe during their visits to the city. To-day it is an hotel where you may live amid splendour and luxury like an eastern potentate, surrounded by gardens whose loveliness must surely transcend the most imaginative vision of Eden.

A multitude of birds sing among its peaceful groves as we pass. Bright coloured butterflies rest trembling amid the flaming blossoms. Silver-green olive groves, ancient as the city walls, give shade and solitude to the weary traveller in the heat of the day; oranges and the great purple sheaths of the banana flower spread their colour on the background of the faded rose walls. Here, after our little trials and tribulations of travelling, we find rest for a while, lying upon cushioned lounges on a Moorish terrace of the hotel as we are served with cooling drinks by a quiet-moving Arab servitor, who ministers to our needs as once the slaves ministered to those of the Sultan's son.

While we are here, let me tell you a story. Across the garden, in the wall that separates us from the desert, there is a small low doorway. Beyond lies the wilderness, with a few camels shuffling away into the sunset, and a *caid* riding into the city, a white figure of magnificence on his black barb. This doorway has a curious history. Many years ago a certain Ambassador, Sir William Kirby Green, came from the Court of Britain upon an unpleasant task. He had to exact an indemnity from the Sultan, whose troops had opposed some English adventurers bent on a strange mission.

They had taken possession of an island at the coast and fortified it as a preliminary to flooding the Sahara and turning it into a lake. It was a fantastic scheme, born of crazy minds, and the Sultan naturally preferred that the desert should remain a desert; but his troops had opposed these men, and the dignity of an all-powerful Britain had been ruffled, and reparation had to be made.

Now the Ambassador was a man well on in years

and none so strong in the heart, and it is said that he became so choleric during his interview with the suave and gracious Sultan that he fell dead of a heart attack on this terrace. His body had to be sent back to England, which was a matter of little difficulty. More difficult was the problem of taking it through the city of Marrakech. The Moslems were in those days not so tolerant of Christians, and it was not fitting that an Unbeliever's corpse should be carried through the streets.

The Sultan solved the problem. He cut that small doorway in the wall, and through it passed the dead Ambassador, out on to the plain and so round the city towards the sea.

The moral of this seems to be that it is better to keep one's temper, even though the losing of it does give one the privilege of having a private door made for one's corpse.

3

To-day we are invited to meet El Hadji Fahmi el Glaoui, paramount Pasha of Marrakech, and one of the three Grand Caids of the Atlas. The others are M'Tougi and Goundafi, but the greatest is the Glaoui. He is a man of whom the people in the south speak almost with bated breath, so fabulous are his riches, so great his power. Men who delight in political machinations envy him his skill in such matters, for it has raised him to a position which gives him an influence greater than that of the Sultan. Those who delight in the pleasures of love envy him his harem, in which it is said there are two hundred women or more. One of his wives, now dead, came to him through a game of cards. He was playing *ecarté* with a Turkish pasha, and the stakes ran so high and his opponent lost so heavily that at last he put up his latest and loveliest Circassian bride in a final effort to retrieve his lost fortune. The Glaoui won her; but with a fine gesture he waived his claim, to the gratification of his rival. He had not reckoned with the lady who had been the trophy. She was a woman of high principles, and insisted that the debt should be honoured.

El Glaoui owns five great palaces in Marrakech. His domains extend far beyond the Atlas mountains into the south. He owns a gold mine, but has not bothered to develop it. The great pass through which we travelled on our way from Ouarzazate belongs to him, and by the skilful use of a few hundred men of his private army of ten thousand he can cut off the Sahara from the north and disorganise the whole of Morocco. In this pass, dominated by the great *kasbah* of Telouet, with its dungeons where men can live and die forgotten, rules his son and heir, the Caid, to whom the Glaoui has delegated many of his privileges and powers.

The French, who call this Pasha the Black Panther, pay great respect to his power and much money into his coffers, for he keeps the peace among the tribes of the south and so liberates many troops who would otherwise be needed for the task. A word from the Glaoui, and the tribes would be in revolt. It was chiefly with his aid that France was able to hold Morocco during the war, when all their soldiers were needed for the fighting fronts. Yet a few years before the war the young Glaoui was fighting the French with all the skill and desperate courage of a Berber chief. His star had not risen high in those days; it was the Great War that gave him his chance to use his political skill by playing the game of the French in Morocco. His father before him was of little account; he is said to have been a mere trader in salt. His mother was a black slave. To-day the son is a feudal chief who lives like Haroun al Raschid, yet has

brokers to do his business on the Stock Exchanges of
Paris, London and New York . . .

The young Arab guide who takes us to the
Glaoui's palace leads us by devious ways until we reach
a street in which towers a high blank wall, windowless
and with an unimposing doorway, at which gathers a
crowd of barbaric-looking men. There are Mokhaznis
with their blue flowing cloaks, brown faced Berbers,
negroes from whose ears hang big silver rings, sign
of their allegiance to the Glaoui. A few saddled mules
are tethered by the wall. The crowd make way
for us, and we enter a long Moorish hall, where
many more retainers stand about awaiting the behest
of their lord. Here we are met by the seneschal of
this feudal baron, a dark-skinned, elderly Berber
of gracious manner, who greets us with quiet words
and leads us into a pillared courtyard which is a
garden, where a fountain plays among orange trees
and the air is fragrant with the delicate perfume of
flowers.

Here stands the Glaoui, talking with two other of
his guests. He advances to greet us and takes our
hands. He is a tall man, six feet or more, and slim.
He is perhaps fifty years of age. He wears the graceful
robes of his race, with a transparent muslin slip over
a pale blue undergarment. He has a dark skin, a tuft
of beard, full lips, and heavy-lidded eyes that shine
brilliantly as he talks in a quiet restrained voice. His
manner is courtly and strangely gentle for a man who
has been a savage fighter and bears the scars of sixteen
wounds on his seemingly frail body.

He asks after our health and whether we have
journeyed comfortably before he introduces us to his
other guests, a colonel and a captain of the French
army. His quiet courtesy and unobtrusive efficiency
as a host at once create an atmosphere of easy
friendliness. He establishes a mutual interest between

ourselves and his military friends by telling them of our journey and mentioning the camps through which we have passed; and so, having given us these points of contact as an opening for conversation, he excuses himself with a deprecatory gesture and goes to superintend the feast.

And presently the seneschal ushers us through another arched doorway, another chamber, and so past golden doorways into a cool Moorish hall where the feast is laid out under the basket covers that always conceal the delights of a Moorish banquet. Beside them stand half a dozen negroes in white with touches of crimson, the slave-ring of the Glaoui in their ears. We take our seats on cushions in a circle at one end of the hall, and the entertainment takes its normal course. It begins with the washing of hands in perfumed water; the low round table is set in our midst; then follows soup in small bowls, the roast chickens, a lamb roasted whole and stuffed with almonds and dates, *couscous* in a great dish, pastries and fruit. The meal differs little from that rich banquet through which we struggled at the house of Youssef ben Tayyib in Fez, so I refrain from describing it in detail. I am more interested in the personality of the Glaoui.

Though he is so pleasant a host, he is unfathomable. He is knowledgeable, he talks with quiet fluency on many subjects in that soft musical voice of his; he tells a story, laughs restrainedly with a genuine humour that shines in his deep-set eyes; yet with it all there is an aloofness about him. He gives us the impression that his thoughts do not coincide with his words. When his face is in repose it has a pensive, almost sorrowful expression, as though he were brooding on the tragedies of the world. It is hard to realise that this man with the delicate movements and gestures is a great warrior; but it is easy to see in him a subtle diplomat, a dangerous enemy and a merciless overlord.

He talks of England, and tells us that he will be visiting London in the summer, after he has been to Paris. Every year now he pays a visit to London. He likes to play golf at Coombe Hill, and has his own golf course outside Marrakech, where he would be happy to see us. He likes to go shopping in Oxford Street and thinks Hyde Park and Kensington Gardens pleasant places worthy of a great capital. He may also revisit Brighton, which he thinks is one of the most graceful towns in the world. With the Frenchman he discusses Paris, telling of the pleasure he finds in his annual visit, and of his son's enthusiasm for the city where he received his education.

So the evening passes in pleasant, intimate talk, while musicians in the outer rooms play strange barbaric little airs; and it is near midnight when we say our farewells to this Sultan of the South in his garden court. We take with us a last impression of the delicate pressure of a hand which in this country wields power in ways that are strange and often unorthodox.

4

You may wander for days in this vivid African city without exhausting its fascination. Its narrow *souks* offer you all the wares of the East. Leather workers and coppersmiths, silversmiths and jewellers, blacksmiths and armourers ply their craft in the small open shops. Or you may find entertainment in the great open space which men call Djemaa el F'na, the Meeting Place of the Dead, where all the variegated races of the south congregate to enjoy life. It was here that in days past the Sultans used to display the heads of captives, traitors and rebels. Some of those ten thousand heads which Moulay Ismail sent to the cities as a proof of his power stared down with sightless eyes on the crowds in the Djemaa el F'na. In this place at evening we hear the sound of many tom-toms, whose insistent rhythms reverberate through the city and over the plain, calling to those who seek entertainment after the stress of the day's work in palace or shop, desert or mountain. Here you will see the conjurors and acrobats, sorcerers and snake-charmers, the wizards and those who cast out devils. Barbers sit beneath oval canopies of woven rush, shaving the heads of the people. Aged and wizened beauty experts crouch in the dust before their scraps of kohl and charcoal, bright coloured unguents and henna for dyeing the feet and hands of women. Daughters of joy, whose golden shoes proclaim their ancient profession, pass in and out of the crowds; they are brown, they are black, they are fair-skinned as an Englishwoman. Dancing-boys who play at being girls perform their sensuous little gyrations to the music of flute and drum, while they ogle the better dressed men among their spectators in search of likely lovers. A long-haired fanatic, shouting wildly, goes prancing and wheeling across our path, followed by the jeers of small boys.

We were standing here one evening watching a conjurer when a voice behind us said in broken English, " Excuse, please, mistah, excuse."

We turned to face a middle-aged Berber in white burnous and hood, whose chin was adorned with a tuft of pointed beard, the fashion of the south.

"Excuse, yes. You know Mistah Bertram Mills, yes?" was his surprising question.

I replied that we did.

"I know, too. I work for him long time ago, yes, London, Bir-*ming*-ham, Glasgow, all over. How Bertram Mills now, all-right and good?"

I told him Bertram Mills was dead.

" Ah. Good man, Bertram Mills. I work for him all over, yes. Acrobat, like that." He pointed with his staff towards a crowd gathered round some performers in the red and yellow garments of the followers of Sidi Ahmed ou Moussa. " I work all over world, yes. Look."

He held out his staff for us to inspect. It was covered with small metal shields representing the theatres and halls at which he had performed. He had been in London and Paris and Berlin, Cologne and Brussels, Vienna and half the cities of Europe. He was proud of his career and his travels, which ended nearly twenty years ago, when he became too old for the business of leaping and twisting and tumbling. He returned to his own country with his savings, lost most of them in business, and now has a Moorish café, to which he invites us.

We walk with him across the crowded, lively Meeting Place of the Dead into the *souks*, and presently we are sitting on mats among his friends, in a cool dim Moorish cavern opening on a narrow street, with glasses of mint tea before us; and musicians who sit on a dais in the background play those high-pitched, leaping jangles of sound that make Moorish music, and sing their doleful stanzas of strange song.

5

It was through our acquaintance with this acrobat that the Spirit had her first experience of harem life. We were invited to the house of one of his friends, a prosperous merchant in leather, and while I sat with the men the Spirit spent the afternoon with the women. Before she entered their quarters she was requested to leave her shoes outside the door, as a warning to the men of the house that there was a strange woman present.

The eldest of the four wives was little more than

thirty, but she was already a grandmother; the youngest was fifteen and a mother. The Spirit told me later that she sat with them eating sweet sticky cake and enjoying the naive curiosity they displayed in her own mode of life. Apparently it was the first time they had entertained a Christian. They displayed an intense interest in our marriage customs, and were surprised to learn that an Englishman could have only one wife at a time, and that he must stay married for life to that one woman unless she gave him good reasons for divorce. The difficulty of divorce, too, was a source of wonder and envy. In Morocco a husband may get rid of his wife by the simple method of saying three times, before witnesses, "Woman, I divorce you. Go back to the house of your father." She then ranks as a widow and is permitted to marry again three months later. Her husband may take her back twice, but after the third period of marriage he cannot retrieve her unless he has been married in the meantime to somebody else and divorced from her. A man is limited by Mahomet's Koranic Law to four wives, but may have as many concubines as he desires; and if he tires of these, he may sell them. These unofficial wives are useful, however, because they do most of the housework.

Girls are married as early as the age of ten or twelve, and before the wedding they are fattened with unlimited quantities of *couscous* and sweet cakes. Slim women offer no attractions to the Arab, who prefers his billows of flesh. When a girl marries, she brings to the husband's home a supply of household goods and furniture, which she can take away if she should be divorced; and the bridegroom makes a money gift to her father. Until they are grandmothers, and therefore considered to have lost most of their attractions, wives must not so much as speak to a man outside the family circle.

But polygamy among the Moors is practised only by the well-to-do; for the poor cannot afford more than one wife. It is a costly business for a man, trying to prevent jealousy among his women. One of these wives who entertained the Spirit explained that when her husband returned from a journey he brought each of them a present; but if he was displeased with one, he omitted the gift. These presents seem to be among the "high spots" in lives that otherwise are excessively dull. The wives of the prosperous Moor have nothing to do but laze, eat, and dream sensual thoughts. Their chief occupation is needlework and embroidery. They have not even the weekly diversion of "going to church" on the Friday Sabbath, for no woman may enter a mosque, since only men are of any account in the eyes of Allah. Women have consolation in the hope of going to Paradise by the performance of good deeds on earth; but even in Paradise they will be given the menial tasks. One of their few diversions on the Sabbath is to visit the graveyards, where you will see them standing about in groups like sheeted ghosts, talking together or meditating over the dead. They are abysmally ignorant of life and the world, and are not encouraged to take an interest in things of the mind. Only one of the Spirit's four hostesses understood French, and this she learned from a concubine, who was so much a woman of the world that she spoke the language fluently . . .

When we left the house of the Merchant, the Spirit was thanking her particular star which had allowed her to be born outside the realms of Islam.

6

We found the café of our acrobat a useful place of call. It was here that we met the slave-dealer. Now officially, under French rule, slavery has been abolished. There are no longer public markets for the buying and selling of human beings. In the past, caravans from the Sahara and the Niger and Sudan used to bring many black slaves through the passes of the Atlas to Marrakech. To-day the business has suffered so great a decline, since it has to be carried on furtively, that the price of slaves has become prohibitive to all but the rich. The black people of the south are still prepared to sell their surplus children, particularly in lean times of famine; and through a dealer acting as agent in Marrakech it is a simple matter to obtain a negro boy or girl as your own property for the equivalent of about £25.

The slave-dealer who frequented the café of the acrobat was a bearded Arab of middle age, a pleasant enough fellow, who came to enjoy his pipe of *kiff* and glass of tea. We were not permitted to discuss slavery in his presence: as foreigners and Christians we could not be trusted. But our acrobat told us that this dealer acted as southern agent for others in Fez, and had the handling of fifty or sixty black slaves in a year.

But slaves, he explained, are not what they used to be. They are an independent lot. Under modern laws, unobtrusively introduced, they can demand to be sold if dissatisfied with their masters; and may even refuse to be bought if they do not approve of their new prospective owner. Things, it appears, are coming to a pretty pass in the slavery business.

Yet it seemed to us, as we sometimes watched a " slave" laughing joyously at the antics of an entertainer in the Djemaa el F'na, that modern slavery is perhaps not so terrible a fate as the propagandists would have us believe. Most of its victims in Marrakech seem to be inordinately happy fellows.

7

We lingered many days in Marrakech, wandering in its gardens beside waters that shone like burnished copper in the sun by day and changed to blue pools of mystery at evening; or exploring the *souks* and the hidden places of the city until we were as familiar with their rambling routes as with the streets at home. But a time came when we had to move on, for the day of Mouloud, the Birthday of the Prophet, draws near, and we had promised to return to Rabat to celebrate.

We discuss modes of travel, and decide to forget the existence of buses. We had achieved our ambition, which was to reach Saharan territory; and we confess to each other that we are a little tired of the racket and the heat of native conveyances. Now Marrakech is the terminus of a magnificent electric railway from the north, and the temptation to use it was too great to be resisted.

The last glimpse we had of the city, as we sped across the brown and purple plain one golden afternoon at sixty miles an hour, was of the red tower of the Koutoubia mosque rising above the palm groves against the blue background of snow-crested Atlas.

CHAPTER 11.

Tells of Revelry in Rabat — the Man who was Mahomet — Garden of Peace — the Legend of the Storks — Pirate City — the Place where Crusoe Slaved — Sultan's Reception — Fantasia with Guns — Lyautey.

I

There is a sound of revelry in Rabat when we awake on the morning of Mouloud, the Christmas Day of the Moslems. From our bedroom balcony we look on a white city whose broad avenues are alive with an unceasing procession of native life. From all parts of the country the people have come to-day to celebrate, and the *caids* and *sheikhs* to swear fealty to the Sultan Moulay Mohammed and bring him gifts. Up and down the avenues they pass, powerful-looking, white-robed, bearded men from the far desert places, from northern cities and barren lands of the south, from oases and mountains; men whose colour ranges from pale parchment to ebony. They crowd the chromium-plated cafés that line our street, taking their sweet coffee and mint tea while they look out on the life of a city which many of them visit only once in a year. A great throbbing of tom-toms rises from below, accompanied by the shrill leaping melodies of the *rheita*, the native flute. The café-garden of the *hotel* under our window is filled with *caids* and *sharifs*, who sit under the orange-coloured sun umbrellas as they take their refreshment.

When we go down, we find a hundred or more of them in the lounge hall of the hotel; and whom should we see but the Glaoui himself, up from his southern domain for the feast. He greets us with the same quiet courtesy with which he received us in his palace. He asks after our health. They are all here to-day, Glaoui, Goundafi, M'Tougi, all the great feudal barons of the south, staying in this hotel which is one of the many possessions of the Glaoui. He built it, we learn, for the accommodation of visitors to the city, and maintains it at considerable loss to his exchequer. But what should that matter to a man who owns a gold mine which he cannot be troubled to develop?

The sunshine strikes at us through a burning-glass when we go out into the streets and walk down to the old town, through the gateway in the yellow-brown wall into the native city, the old Rabat of the Moors. Everywhere are the sounds and sights of festival. Houses have been newly whitewashed; even the ground at the sides of the alleyways that are streets have their coat of white for this day. Arab children, dressed in their best, are enjoying the holiday in the manner of children, sucking enormous sweets and toffees of violent hue. The little girls wear their best muslins, and their hair is crimped and curled and pigtailed in the parts where it has not been shaved. At the doors of houses the white-clad Moorish musicians play to the occupants with tom-tom and flute, so that the streets echo with their shrill, exciting melodies. The wailing cry of the *muezzins* float down from the towers of the mosques, calling the Faithful to the noon-day prayer; men leave their work and hurry away to worship Allah the one God . . .

Since this is the birthday of Mahomet, perhaps I will be forgiven if I digress to consider what manner of man was this inspired camel-driver who conceived a religion that holds half the world. His full name was Mahomet ibn Abdallah ibn Abdal Muttalib ibn Hashim. They say that soon after he was born at Mecca in 570 A.D., he showed signs of epilepsy; but that the symptoms passed with childhood and he developed into a good-looking young man, quiet and pleasant in manner and honest in his dealings, so that men called him al-Amin, the reliable. As a cameleer he made many journeys into Syria and the Yemen in the service of his uncle, and took part in the tribal wars of the Bedouins. When he was twenty-five he entered the business of a rich widow named Khadija, who three years later offered herself in marriage to him "because of his loyalty and honesty and good life." She belonged to a noble Meccan family, and her father refused consent to the union; so Khadija made him drunk, obtained his blessing before he sobered, and by a similar trick induced her uncle to mumble the marriage formula. Henceforth Mahomet lived the life of a prosperous merchant; but this in no way changed his character. He had always liked the pleasant things of living. Agreeable perfumes, women and prayer, he said, were the most beautiful things in life. He used pomades and scents, and anointed his long-lashed dark eyes to brighten them. His black perfumed hair he wore in two plaits. He washed frequently, and constantly chewed bark to keep his teeth white. He disliked over-eating, drinking, or any kind of indulgence.

In middle age he began to be tortured by doubts, neglected his business, became a hermit, and out of his mental turmoil and the visions to which it gave birth, he produced the first chapters of the Koran. Through persecution he spread the new faith of Islam, the doctrine of submission to the will of the one God. His rise to power in Medina did not spoil him. He lived simply, gave to the poor, mended his own clothes, and helped to build the first mosque, carrying the clay and making the bricks. After the death of Khadija he abandoned monogamy and in the course of time took fourteen wives, with each of whom he spent a night in turn. Each had her own clay hut; Mahomet had no house of his own. He taught his followers that Believers who died for the cause of Islam went to a paradise of sensual delights, where they would be tended by dark-eyed houris and youths who were for ever young. He destroyed the worship of idols and substituted belief in one God, in pre-destination, in the Prophet, in the equality of man and in a life hereafter. He imposed the four duties — of prayer five times a day, fasting, the giving of alms, and pilgrimage to Mecca. On these foundations he built a faith which so inspired his desert race that within a few centuries they had created an Empire that has had few equals in the history of the ancient world.

Thus was the man whose birthday we are celebrating to-day as we wander through Rabat . . .

Soon we mount a slope and come to the great ochre-tinted gateway to the *kasbah*, and beside it a smaller gateway that leads us into the Garden of the Oudaias. Now of all the gardens in Morocco this surely must be the most beautiful. It stands on the site of a palace build by a great sultàn, el Mansur the Golden, who brought stores of gold from Timbuktu and spent much of it in beautifying his domain with mosques and colleges. Ochre-rose walls four feet high surround this garden, where trees droop their burdens of oranges and citrons and bananas in the sun amid massed screens of purple bougainvillaea and blue volubilis. We walk under pergolas of vine through colours more vivid than any conceived in an artist's dream. At one end of the garden, on a terrace where goldfish dart among floating lilies in a pool, a blind-fold donkey harnessed to a primitive wooden wheel plods in an eternal circle, drawing water from a well. Behind him rises a building with a square tower, the colour of burnt sienna. It was once part of a school for piracy in the bad old days of the Barbary corsairs. A multitude of storks perch on the crenelated walls, clattering their long beaks as they watch over their ungainly nests.

There is good reason for this clatter, so legend tells. The first storks were once upon a time a man and woman. The man was rich in flocks and grain and lived in a fine house. A time came when there was famine in the land, and food was so scarce and dear that the poor could not afford to buy. Now this rich man, like so many of his kind, was not rich enough for his liking, so he conceived a plan to gain even more money.

He went into the city and cried to the people, " Come, all ye who wish to buy grain, to my house. Bring only half as much money as thou wouldst pay for grain in the market place, and thou shalt have all thou needest."

Then the rich man returned to his house and bade his servant prepare soap and fill it with pieces of broken glass, and put it by until after the people had been to buy again. When the buyers came, they were sent upstairs to the rich man, and bought all they desired, and paid the price. And while they were transacting their business, the servant went in secret and smeared upon the stairs the soap and glass which he had prepared at the bidding of his lord. When the poor men came from the rich man's chamber, the rich man waxed angry with them, crying, " Get ye gone, get ye gone from my house," and set about them with a staff, so that in their hurry to go they slipped on the soap and glass and fell to the bottom of the stairs, spilling the grain they had bought.

And when they had been driven from the house, the rich man and his wife stood upon the stairs laughing at their discomfort; and while they laughed Allah turned them into storks as a punishment, depriving them of the power of speech, and granting them no more than this cackling laugh which we hear from the walls of the garden . . .

Through another gateway, and we are in a Moorish café, where *caids* and *khalifas* sit over their tea in the shade of vines, on a cliff above the blue waters of the Bou Regreg, the Father of Shining. While we sit here on a wall-seat we look across to the far shore, to the white towers and walls of Salé, the old pirate city. Into this port in past centuries came many an unfortunate Englishman, chained in some ship of the " Sallee rovers" to be sold into slavery. Here came many of the thousands of captives who worked out their miserable lives in the brutal service of Moulay Ismail at Meknes. From this town the Barbary pirates set out to scour the seas for treasure and raid the coasts of Britain and France and Spain for slaves. Robinson Crusoe spent two years here in slavery . . .

"Our ship making her course towards the Canary Islands, was surprised in the grey of the morning by a rover of Sallee, who gave chase to us with all the sail she could make," says Crusoe.

After a desperate fight he and his companions were captured and " carried all prisoners into Sallee, a port belonging to the Moors. Here I was kept by the captain of the rover, as his proper prize, and made his slave, being young and nimble, and fit for his business."

If you will turn to Defoe, you will read how Crusoe escaped by throwing overboard the unfortunate Moor who used to accompany him on fishing expeditions in his master's boat, and sailed away down the coast of Africa to new adventures. The same " castle at the entrance to the port" of which he speaks can be seen from where we sit . . .

In this pleasant manner, wandering amid the beauty and colour of the old city, we spend the morning of Mouloud until it is time to drive to the

Palace for the Sultan's reception. We clatter up the hill through the new city of Lyautey in a barouche which is one of hundreds, all carrying *caids* and veiled women and army officers. Through a gateway in the outer walls we emerge on to a walled plateau above the sea. At the far end, half a mile away, the Sultan's Palace spreads itself in a line of low white buildings, with towers and balconies and wide arched entrances. A vast multitude fills this plateau. There are veiled women, children in bright blues and greens, rich Arabs, wild Berbers, beggars and thieves, all come for their day of entertainment. They gather in great crowds around the thousand and one entertainers. Here are snake-charmers and dancers, singers and wizards, drinkers of boiling water and fire-eaters, fuzzy-headed negro musicians from the Sudan, holy dervishes from the south. Vendors of sweetmeats and great sticky cakes offer their delights to women who cannot enjoy because they may not unveil their faces, but most carry away their purchases until they reach some secluded place where they can eat. There must be fifty thousand people congregated here in front of the Palace.

Our carriage puts us down at one of the entrances, where giant negroes of the Sultan's Black Guard bar further progress. They wear crimson costumes with baggy trousers of the plus-four type and red turbans set with white diamond-shaped patches. A French official meets us, receives our card, and leads us across to one of a pair of canvas pavilions erected beside the Palace. In one are gathered the élite of Rabat, the officials and their wives; in the other, servants are feverishly preparing for the arrival of the Resident General and his staff. The reception tent is by no means ready; but then few things in Morocco are ever ready in time. Servants stagger out of the Palace with long rolls of Moorish carpet, which they drop at the

entrance to the pavilion. Suffocating clouds of dust
rise from these carpets, drawing from the Spirit —
when she has finished coughing — the comment that
the Palace should offer a fair field for a vacuum-
cleaner salesman.

When the carpets are laid and we are seated, there
is a commotion in the vast white-robed throng as a
contingent of Black Guards come marching across the
plateau, to the music of squealing flutes and throbbing
drums. They part the crowds and head them away
from the Palace, leaving an open space some two
hundred yards long and a hundred wide. Then a line
of cars approaches, and General Nogues with his staff
alight and take their seats in the pavilion. A crowd
of Moors come across from the Palace, escorting the
Grand Vizier, a white-robed elderly man, who greets
the General and sits beside him.

And now there is a great marching of Black
Guards, and a piping and a drumming, as these
magnificent fellows in their bright reds and blues
display their pride, following behind a drum-major
black as coal and big as Goliath, who whirls a great
baton around his head, performing miracles of
dexterity. They range themselves on one side of the
square, facing the pavilions, to await their Lord
the Sultan.

We are expectant, we are on tip-toe, watching for
a brilliant cavalcade. But suddenly there is a flurry of
small hooves, and from the Palace entrance comes a
tiny governess car drawn by two Shetland ponies.
It is driven by a prim, spectacled Frenchwoman.
Beside her sit two very small boys in the uniforms of
colonels: the Sultan's heir and his brother, the prim
lady their governess. The first shock of surprise gives
place to a ripple of delighted laughter and many
French exclamations of pleasure. Across the open
space comes this toy parade, while the drums thunder

and the pipes squeal and the multitude send up that strange, shrilling applause of tongue-on-lips which we first heard at the wedding feast at Tinerhir: a weird and thrilling sound when it comes from ten thousand mouths. The car draws up before the pavilion, and the future Sultan and his brother alight, turn right and left with stiff little bows like the movements of marionettes, and take their places beside the Vizier and the Resident General.

Next comes the Sultan himself, emerging from the Palace on a pale gold steed led by two grooms and surrounded by many retainers. A court official holds above him on a long stem the green Imperial Umbrella, symbol of the Sultanate, the Shadow of God on Earth. Except for this umbrella and the red caps of the retainers, the *motif* is white. The Sultan sits straight and slim on his horse, his white robe covering him like a sheet from head to foot, only his pale brown face visible.

On his horse he is led into the centre of the open space, and there stays, impassive, magnificent in his simplicity.

At the far end of the arena the *caids* have gathered. At a signal the first group of them advances in a long line, a score of men of fine stature and great dignity of bearing. Before the Sultan they halt, bowing low to the ground. Then one of the Sultan's officials calls out in a loud voice, demanding their fealty. Again they bow low, answering in well-rehearsed unison. Three times they make their bows before they back away and eliminate themselves, giving place to another line of advancing *caids* who go through the same ceremony.

Each line as it advances is accompanied on one flank by servants of the Sultan, leading horses and mules laden with big white paste-board boxes. These boxes, with the animals that carry them, are the gifts of the *caids* to their Lord. They look to be such splendid presents, and we speculate on what mysteries the boxes may contain. What kind of a present does a *caid* give to his Sultan? Precious stones, silver and gold, weapons of rare workmanship? We ask a certain French official who is our companion, and he whispers disillusionment in our ears. Many of the *caids* are poor, he says, and cannot always afford to give presents; so that some of the boxes are empty, or else they have been filled by one of the officials of the Court. As for the horses, those splendid white chargers and well-groomed mules, — well, it is not unknown, says he, for them to have been brought from the Sultan's stables and returned to him as gifts.

When all the *caids* have paid their homage, and the pipes are squealing again and the drums beating, the Sultan's horse is turned and led back to the Palace. And still that silent figure under the Imperial Umbrella has given no sign of life. He disappears through the wide entrance to his Palace, surrounded by his retainers, and followed by the shrill applause of the watching multitude.

And now begins the real excitement of the reception, the *fantasia* or power play. At the end of the open space a crowd of horsemen congregate, wild-looking, fierce fellows, the best riders in Morocco. A dozen of them line up, and at a signal they come charging across the plain, whirling their guns in the air. As they approach the Palace their leader gives a cry and every gun is fired into the air. So perfect is the timing that the volley sounds as one shot. Applause shrills from the spectators. The horsemen veer away, and a second line comes on, then a third and a fourth in rapid succession. Sometimes the volley is ragged and broken, and we hear the leader cursing his followers as they move off; but at times you would swear, if you had not been watching, that no more than one gun had been fired. For half an hour these charges continue, until the multitude begins to melt away in search of other distractions. The Resident General departs with his staff, the pavilions are cleared, and the people are left to the enjoyment of their *fête*. The Sultan's reception is over, but the gigantic party goes on until nightfall.

And then there is feasting and music through the ancient city, and children dance in the narrow streets to the leaping melodies of serenaders; until Mahomet's birthday passes with the midnight hour, and Arab, Berber and negro seek their rest on such couches and in such homes as Allah has thought fit to grant them.

2

And now we come to the end of the journey. A train to Tangier, a boat, and we shall be on our way back to reality. But we go with reluctance, for we are abandoning a peace and a simplicity hard to find in the life of the cities we call civilised. We shall take with us the memory of many pleasant encounters and many fantastic scenes; of new friendships that seem somehow to give us an anchorage in this land of barbaric beauty and ancient culture. We shall take also a little knowledge of the manners and customs of the people whose mode of life we have learned to respect, and a store of new experiences of a kind that will create in our memories a refuge to which it will always be pleasant to retreat.

Before we go, I should like to take you up the hill above Rabat to a small white building with a green-tiled roof, not unlike the *koubba* of a Moroccan saint. It stands alone in gardens where peace dwells, and where birds sing, and palms and flowers luxuriate in the African sun. It is the tomb of the man who brought Morocco to the French and made its people his friends; who was not only a soldier but a diplomat, a wise administrator and, above all, a man of great heart and deep humanity. Above his resting place you will read this inscription, which he composed himself:

Here Rests
HUBERT GONZAGUE LYAUTEY
Born a Christian, Died a Christian
who wished to rest in this
Moroccan earth among his
Moslem Brothers whom He had
Loved So Much.

THE END.

AFTERWORD

If you read Gordon West's *Jogging Round Majorca* before you came to *By Bus To The Sahara*, you'll know how I discovered that first book of his to be re-published by Black Swan following the success of my BBC Radio 4 abridgement and readings. You'll also recall my keenness to find out something about the man, and how difficult that proved.

But now, with continued help from Huw Molseed of the Book Information Service of the independent educational charity Book Trust, I can tell you more about the man whose writings are giving pleasure to a new generation of readers and who is now a posthumous best-selling author.

Gordon West was born in Guildford on 7 March 1896, son of James (a landowner) and Margaret (Hope) West. He was educated at Guildford Grammar School and the London School of Economics, and served in the Royal Navy during the First World War.

His journalistic career took him from Foreign Correspondent of the *Westminster Gazette* (1926/27) to Editor of *Advertising World* (1929/30), to Foreign Editor of the *Daily Sketch* (1941/45); and he contributed to the *Daily Mail* and *Daily Express* as well as to other newspapers and magazines.

Politically he declared himself a Liberal (for his religion he gave agnostic) and at one time he was editor of publications and acting director of propaganda for the Liberal Party in England. In 1928 he toured the United States with presidential candidates Alfred E. Smith (Democrat) and Herbert Hoover (Republican, who won and served as President of the U.S. from '29 to '33) in order to study election methods for David Lloyd George, who, when *Jogging*

Round Majorca appeared in 1929, was quoted in the publisher's blurb as follows: "This vivid and delightfully written travel book has given me hours of lively entertainment, and much information. The author carries the reader on his journey with a joyous sense of humour, strong powers of observation, and a keen zest for life."

In case you think Lloyd George might have been biased, I should point out that *Jogging* was also enthusiastically welcomed by among others the *Daily Herald, John o'London's Weekly, Sunday Dispatch, Daily Mirror, The People, Birmingham Gazette, Hereford Journal*, and the *Daily Telegraph*, which I'm happy to say was equally welcoming to the 1994 reprint.

You'll have formed your own picture of The Spirit of Joy (his wife Mary, née Coghlan, who signed her paintings Mary Gordon West) and of course the man himself, who listed his interests as "swimming, laughing at life". But although we know from *Jogging* that they had a dog, I wasn't prepared for his admitting to be "an enthusiastic felinophile with a passion for cats (has six); taught one to respond to words in three languages representing objects of special interest to cats."

He was a member of the Place Names Society of Great Britain (researching origins), and a smoker whose writings also included 'The History of Smoking from Elizabeth I to Elizabeth II', 'All About Cigars', and 'All About Pipes'; in fact there's a wonderful photograph of him and Georges Simenon pipe-smoking at the annual dinner of the Briar Pipe Trade Association. I was shown it by Laurence Ridgway, a friend and colleague and one of the only two people at Gordon West's funeral.

The Wests had no children and as is clear from the travel writings were a very self-contained couple, so not surprisingly he was devastated when she died and thereafter spent nearly all his time in The Savage Club, from whose Secretary I learned that Gordon West died on 13 August 1969.

In time, with the help of book searches like London's Travel Bookshop and Fowey's Book Ends who found me an original copy each of this book, I hope to read all his other works; but there's one that I simply cannot trace, and that's what is listed in his '63/64 c.v. as his first travel book, *Ambling in Albania*, published by Alston Rivers in 1926. The British Museum can't help, neither can The Bodleian or the Cambridge University Library, nor The Royal Geographical or Anglo-Albanian Societies. Can you?

By the way, if my opening "if" was wrong, and you haven't yet read *Jogging Round Majorca*, you have another treat in store.

LEONARD PEARCEY